The Mortification of Sin

A Puritan's View of How to Deal with
Sin in Your Life

John Owen

Introduction by J I Packer

CHRISTIAN HERITAGE

Introduction © J I Packer

ISBN 1-85792-107-0
ISBN 978-1-85792-107-6

10 9 8 7 6 5 4 3 2 1

First published by Christian Focus in 1996,
Reprinted in 2002, 2003, 2006
by
Christian Focus Publications Ltd,
Geanies House, Fearn, Tain, Ross-shire,
IV20 1TW, Scotland

You can now buy online at
www.christianfocus.com

Cover Design by Alister MacInnes

Printed and bound by
Nørhaven Paperback A/S, Denmark

Contents

INTRODUCTION

I owe more, I think, to John Owen than to any other theologian, ancient or modern, and I am sure I owe more to his little book on mortification than to anything else he wrote. Let me explain.

I was converted – that is, I came to the Lord Jesus Christ in a decisive commitment, needing and seeking God's pardon and acceptance, conscious of Christ's redeeming love for me and his personal call to me – in my first university term, a little more than half a century ago. The group nurturing me was heavily pietistic in style, and left me in no doubt that the most important thing for me as a Christian was the quality of my walk with God: in which, of course, they were entirely right. They were also, however, somewhat elitist in spirit, holding that only Bible-believing evangelicals could say anything worth hearing about the Christian life, and the leaders encouraged the rest of us to assume that anyone thought sound enough to address the group on this theme was sure to be good. I listened with great expectation and excitement to the preachers and teachers whom the group brought in week by week, not doubting that they were the top devotional instructors in Britain, perhaps in the world. And I came a cropper.

Whether what I thought I heard was what was really being said may be left an open question, but it seemed to me that what I was being told was this. There are two sorts of Christians, first-class and second-class, 'spiritual' and 'carnal' (a distinction drawn from the King James rendering of 1 Cor. 3:1-3). The former know sustained peace and joy, constant inner confidence, and regular victory over temptation and sin, in a way that the latter do not. Those who hope to be of use to God must become 'spiritual' in the stated sense. As a lonely, nervy, adolescent introvert whose new-found assurance had not changed his temperament overnight, I had to conclude that I was not 'spiritual' yet. But I wanted to be useful to God. So what was I to do?

'Let go, and let God'

There is a secret, I was told, of rising from carnality to spirituality, a secret mirrored in the maxim: Let go, and let God. I vividly recall a radiant clergyman in an Oxford pulpit enforcing this. The secret had to do with being Spirit-filled. The Spirit-filled person, it was said, is taken out of the second half of Romans 7, understood (misunderstood, I would now maintain) as an analysis of constant moral defeat through self-reliance, into Romans 8, where he walks confidently in the Spirit and is not so defeated. The way to be Spirit-filled, so I gathered, was as follows.

First, one must *deny self*. Did not Jesus require self-denial from his disciples (Luke 9:23)? Yes, but clearly what he meant was the negating of carnal self – that is to say self-will, self-assertion, self-centredness and self-worship, the Adamic syndrome in human nature, the egocentric behaviour pattern, rooted in anti-God aspirations and attitudes, for which the common name is original sin. What I seemed to be hearing, however, was a call to deny *personal* self, so that I could be taken over by Jesus Christ in such a way that my present experience of thinking and willing would become something different, an experience of Christ himself living in me, animating me, and doing the thinking and willing for me. Put like that, it sounds more like the formula of demon-possession than the ministry of the indwelling Christ according to the New Testament. But in those days I knew nothing about demon-possession, and what I have just put into words seemed to be the plain meaning of 'I live; yet not I, but Christ liveth in me' (Gal. 2:20, KJV) as expounded by the approved speakers. We used to sing this chorus:

> O to be saved from myself, dear Lord,
> O to be lost in thee;
> O that it may be no more I
> But Christ who lives in me!

Whatever its author may have meant, I sang it whole-heartedly in the sense spelled out above.

The rest of the secret was bound up in the double-barrelled phrase *consecration and faith*. Consecration meant total self-surrender, laying one's all on the altar, handing over every part of one's life to the lordship of Jesus. Through consecration one would be emptied of self, and the empty vessel would then automatically be filled with the Spirit so that Christ's power within one would be ready for use. With consecration was to go faith, which was explained as looking to the indwelling Christ moment by moment, not only to do one's thinking and choosing in and for one, but also to do one's fighting and resisting of temptation. Rather then meet temptation directly (which would be fighting in one's own strength), one should hand it over to Christ to deal with, and look to him to banish it. Such was the consecration-and-faith technique as I understood it – heap powerful magic, as I took it to be, the precious secret of what was called victorious living.

But what happened? I scraped my inside, figuratively speaking, to ensure that my consecration was complete, and laboured to 'let go and let God' when temptation made its presence felt. At that time I did not know that Harry Ironside, sometime pastor of Moody Memorial Church, Chicago, once drove himself into a full-scale mental breakdown through trying to get into the higher life as I was trying to get into it; and I would not have dared to conclude, as I have concluded since, that this higher life as described is a will-o'-the-wisp, an unreality that no one has ever laid hold of at all, and that those who testify to their experience in these terms really, if unwittingly, distort what has happened to them. All I knew was that the expected experience was not coming. The technique was not working. Why not? Well, since the teaching declared that everything depends on consecration being total, the fault had to lie in me. So I must scrape my inside again to find whatever maggots of unconsecrated selfhood still lurked there. I became fairly frantic.

And then (thank God) the group was given an old clergyman's library, and in it was an uncut set of Owen, and I cut the pages of volume VI more or less at random, and read Owen on mortification – and God used what the old Puritan had written three centuries before to sort me out.

A Puritan Giant

Owen was by common consent the weightiest Puritan theologian, and many would bracket him with John Calvin and Jonathan Edwards as one of the three greatest Reformed theologians of all time. Born in 1616, he entered Queen's College, Oxford, at the age of twelve and secured his M.A. in 1635, when he was nineteen. In his early twenties, conviction of sin threw him into such turmoil that for three months he could scarcely utter a coherent word on anything; but slowly he learned to trust Christ, and so found peace. In 1637 he became a pastor; in the 1640s he was chaplain to Oliver Cromwell, and in 1651 he was made Dean of Christ Church, Oxford's largest college. In 1652 he was given the additional post of Vice-Chancellor of the University, which he then reorganized with conspicuous success. After 1660 he led the Independents through the bitter years of persecution till his death in 1683.

He was a conservative Reformed theologian of great learning and expository strength. His thoughts are like the pillars of a Norman cathedral; they leave an impression of massive grandeur precisely because of their solid simplicity. He wrote for readers who, once they take up a subject, cannot rest till they see to the bottom of it, and who find exhaustiveness of coverage and presentation of the same truths from many different angles not exhausting but refreshing. His books have been truly described as a series of theological systems, each organized round a different centre. The truth of the Trinity – the story of the triune Creator becoming the triune Redeemer – was always his final point of reference, and the living of the Christian life was his constant concern.

Owen embodied all that was noblest in Puritan devotion. 'Holiness gave a divine lustre to his other accomplishments,' said his former junior colleague, David Clarkson, preaching at Owen's funeral. As a preacher, Owen bowed before his own maxim, that 'a man preacheth that sermon only well unto others which preacheth itself in his own soul', and declared: 'I hold myself bound in conscience and in honour, not even to imagine that I have attained a proper knowledge of any one article of truth, much less to publish it, unless through the Holy Spirit I have had such a taste of it, in its spiritual sense, that I may be able, from the heart, to say with the psalmist, "I have believed, and therefore have I spoken".' This explains the authority and skill with which Owen probes the dark depths of the human heart. 'Whole passages flash upon the mind of the reader with an influence that makes him feel as if they had been written for himself alone' (Andrew Thomson). The treatise on mortification is a signal example of this.

Wisdom on Mortification

Owen's 'discourse', as he called it, is a written-up set of pastoral sermons on Romans 8:13, KJV, 'If ye through the Spirit do mortify the deeds of the body ye shall live.' The sermons were preached in Oxford and the work was published in 1656 (second enlarged edition, 1658). It has been said of Jane Austen's novels that they should be read first for the fourth time, meaning that only fourth time around will their special excellences of balanced structure, gentle satire and subtle humour come into focus in the reader's mind. The same could be said of these sermons, for only through repeated reading is their searching power and unction adequately felt. Their theme is the negative side of God's work of sanctification (that is, character renewal in Christ's image). Reformed teachers from Calvin on have regularly explained the Holy Spirit's sanctifying work in terms of the positive, vivification (developing virtues), and the negative, mortification (killing sins). As the Westminster Confession (13:1) puts it:

They, who are once effectually called, and regenerated, having a new heart, and a new spirit created in them, are further sanctified, really and personally, through the virtue of Christ's death and resurrection, by his Word and Spirit dwelling in them: the dominion of the whole body of sin is destroyed, and the several lusts thereof are more and more weakened and mortified, and they more and more quickened and strengthened in all saving graces, to the practice of true holiness, without which no man shall see the Lord.

Mortification is Owen's subject, and he is resolved to explain from Scripture the theology of it – that is, God's will, wisdom, work and ways regarding it – as fully as he can. But to make his treatment as practical and useful as possible, he addresses within the frame of his text the following question:

Suppose a man to be a true believer, and yet finds in himself a powerful indwelling sin, leading him captive to the law of it, consuming his heart with trouble, perplexing his thoughts, weakening his soul as to duties of communion with God, disquieting him as to peace, and perhaps defiling his conscience and exposing him to hardening through the deceitfulness of sin, – what shall he do? what course shall he take and insist on for the mortification of this sin, lust, distemper or corruption...?

He then arranges his material as a series of things to know, and things to do, which between them answer the question as posed.

I spoke earlier of how Owen saved my spiritual sanity. I do in fact think, after fifty years, that Owen has contributed more than anyone else to make me as much of a moral, spiritual and theological realist as I have so far become. He searched me to the root of my being. He taught me the nature of sin, the need to fight it and the method of doing so. He made me see the importance of the thoughts of the heart in one's spiritual life. He made clear to me the real nature of the Holy Spirit's ministry in and to the believer, and of spiritual growth and progress, and of faith's victory. He showed me how to understand myself as a Christian and live before God humbly and honestly, without pretending either to be what I am not or not to be what I am. And he made every point by direct biblical exegesis, bringing out the experimental implications of didactic and narrative texts with a precision and profundity that I had not met before, and have rarely seen equalled since. The decisive dawning of all the insight I have ever received from Owen came, however, when first I read him on mortification. This small work is a spiritual gold mine. I cannot commend it highly enough.

Tuning In

I realise, however, as I write this that some readers will find it hard to tune in, so to speak, on Owen's wavelength, not just because his stately Latinized English with its fulsome rhetoric and occasional odd word trips them up, but because they suffer from the shortcomings of much present-day Christian nurture. Four of these in particular call for mention here.

First, *the holiness of God* is insufficiently emphasized. In Scripture, and in Owen, the holiness of 'the holy one' is constantly underlined. Holiness, which has been called the attribute of all God's attributes, is the quality that sets the Creator apart from his creatures, making him different from us in our weakness, awesome and adorable to us in his strength, and a visitant to our consciences whose presence exposes and condemns sin within us. Too often today, however, God's holiness is played down, with the result that his love and mercy are sentimentalized and we end up thinking of him as we would think of a kindly uncle. One effect of this unrealism is to make it hard for us to believe that the holy God of the Bible writers – prophets, psalmists, historians, apostles and very clearly the Lord Jesus Christ himself – is the real God with whom we really have to deal. But the Puritans believed this, and an adjustment here must be made in our minds if we are to understand Owen's theology.

Second, *the significance of motivating desire* is insufficiently emphasized. In Scripture, and in Owen, desire is the index of one's heart, and the motivation is the decisive test of whether actions are good or bad. If the heart is wrong, lacking reverence, or love, or purity, or humility, or a forgiving spirit, but instead festering with pride, self-seeking ambition, envy, greed, hatred, sexual lust or the like, nothing that one does can be right in God's sight, as Jesus told the Pharisees time and time again. Too often today, however, as among the Pharisees, the moral life is reduced to role-play, in which prescribed and expected performance is everything and no attention is paid to the craving, ragings and hostilities of the heart so long as people do what it is thought they should. This externalism, however, by which we assess ourselves, is not God's way of assessing us, and when Scripture tells Christians to mortify sin, the meaning is not just that bad habits must be broken, but that sinful desires and urgings must have the life drained out of them – which is what Owen is concerned to help us with throughout his book. An adjustment of outlook must be made here too if we are to understand Owen's thrust.

Third, *the need for self-scrutiny* is insufficiently emphasized. In Scripture, and in Owen, much stress is laid on the deceitfulness of the fallen human heart, and the danger of self-ignorance, with the result that one thinks well of one's heart and life when God, the searcher of hearts, is displeased with both. It is supremely ironical that in an era in which professional mind-doctors make so much of hidden and unrealized motivations, Christians should so regularly and resolutely decline to suspect themselves or each other of any form of self-deception in their ideas about themselves. Owen, a Puritan realist, knows that we are constantly fooling ourselves, or being fooled, with regard to our real attitudes and purposes, and hence insists that we must watch and examine ourselves by Scripture in order even to know what habits of our hearts need to be mortified. An adjustment in our mind-set has to be made here also if we are to understand Owen's probings.

Fourth, *the life-changing power of God* is insufficiently emphasized. In Scripture, and in Owen, subjective salvation means in the most literal sense a change of heart: a moral change that is rooted in a sustained exercise of faith, hope and love, whereby the power of Christ's death to deliver from domination by sinful desire, and the power of the Holy Spirit to induce Christlike attitudes and actions are constantly being proved. Mistaken as was the formula for supernatural living from which Owen delivered me, the expectation that Christians through prayer to Jesus would know deliverances from sinful passions in the heart was wholly right, and it is sad – indeed, scandalous – that today so little is heard about this, when so much is said about the power of Christ and his Spirit in various forms of ministry. But real deliverance from sinful passions is the blessing into which Owen would lead us, and he does not doubt that it is there to be had. 'Set faith at work on Christ for the *killing* of thy sin,' he writes. 'His blood is the great sovereign remedy for sin-sick souls. Live in this, and thou wilt die a conqueror; yea, thou wilt, through the good providence of God, live to see thy lust dead at thy feet.' Here, once more, an adjustment of our interest and expectancy must be made if we are to benefit from Owen's guidance.

Read on, then, with readiness to learn of the power of your Saviour and his Holy Spirit to set you free from your particular bondages to inordinate desire. God give us all hearts to understand and apply the truths that Owen sets forth here.

J I Packer

CHAPTER 1

The foundation of the whole ensuing discourse laid in Romans 8:13. The words of the apostle opened. The certain connection between true mortification and salvation. Mortification the work of believers. The Spirit the principal efficient cause of it. What meant by 'the body' in the words of the apostle. What by 'the deeds of the body'. Life, in what sense promised to this duty.

That what I have of direction to contribute to he carrying on the work of mortification in believers, may receive order and perspicuity, I shall lay the foundation of it in those words of the apostle (Rom. 8:13), 'If ye through the Spirit do mortify the deeds of the body, ye shall live'; and reduce the whole to an improvement of the great evangelical truth and mystery contained in them.

The apostle having made a recapitulation of his doctrine of justification by faith, and the blessed estate and condition of them who are made by grace partakers thereof (vv. 1-3 of this chapter), proceeds to improve it, to the holiness and consolation of believers.

Among his arguments and motives unto holiness, the verse mentioned containeth one, from the contrary events and effects of holiness and sin: 'if ye live after the flesh, ye shall die'. What it is to 'live after the flesh', and what it is to 'die', that being not my present aim and business, I shall no otherwise explain than as they will fall in with the sense of the latter words of the verse, as before proposed.

In the words peculiarly designed for the foundation of the ensuing discourse, there is, first, a duty prescribed: 'mortify the deeds of the body'; secondly, the persons are denoted to whom it is prescribed: 'ye, if ye mortify'; thirdly, there is in them a promise annexed to that duty: 'ye shall live'; fourthly, the cause or means of the performance of this duty, the Spirit: 'if ye through the Spirit'; fifthly, the conditionality of the whole proposition, wherein duty, means and promise are contained: 'if ye', etc.

But as the words lie in the entire proposition,

(1) The first thing occurring in the conditional note, 'but if'. Conditionals in such propositions may denote two things:

(i) The uncertainty of the event or thing promised, in respect of them to whom the duty is prescribed. And this takes place where the condition is absolutely necessary unto the issue, and depends not itself on any determinate cause known to him to whom it is prescribed. So we say, 'If we live we will do such a thing.' This cannot be the intention of the conditional expression in this place. Of the persons to whom these words are spoken, it is said, verse 1 of the same chapter, 'there is no condemnation to them'.

(ii) The certainty of the coherence and connection that is between the things spoken of: as we say to a sick man, 'If you will take such a potion, or use such a remedy, you will be well': the thing we solely intend to express, is the certainty of the connection that is between the potion or remedy and health. And this is the use of it here. The certain connection that is between the 'mortifying of the deeds' of the body, and 'living', is intimated in this conditional particle.

Now the connection and coherence of things being manifold, as of cause and effect, of way and means and the end; this, between mortification and life, is not of cause and effect properly and strictly, for 'eternal life is the gift of God through Jesus Christ' (Rom. 6:23); but of means and end: God hath appointed this means, for the attaining that end which he hath freely promised. Means, though necessary, have a fair subordination to an end of free promise. A gift, and a procuring cause in him to whom it is given, are inconsistent. The intention, then, of this proposition as conditional is, *That there is a certain infallible connection and coherence between true mortification and eternal life.* If you use this means, you shall obtain that end. If you do 'mortify' you shall live. And herein lies the main motive unto, and enforcement of, the duty prescribed.

(2) The next thing we meet with in the words is the persons to whom this duty is prescribed, and that is

expressed in the word 'ye', if 'ye mortify'; that is, ye believers; ye to whom 'there is no condemnation' (v. 1); ye that are not in the flesh, but in the Spirit (v. 5); who are 'quickened by the Spirit of Christ' (vv. 10, 11); to you is this duty prescribed. The pressing of this duty immediately on any other is a notable fruit of that superstition and self-righteousness that the world is so full of: the great work and design of devout men ignorant of the gospel (Rom. 10:3, 4; John 15:5). Now, this description of the persons, in conjunction with the prescription of the duty, is the main foundation of the ensuing discourse, as it lies in this thesis or proposition: *The choicest believers, who are assuredly freed from the condemning power of sin, ought yet to make it their business, all their days, to mortify the indwelling power of sin.*

(3) The principal efficient *cause* of the performance of this duty is the Spirit: 'if by the Spirit'. The Spirit here, is the Spirit mentioned (v. 11), the 'Spirit of Christ', the Spirit of God that dwells in us (v. 9), that quickens us (v. 11), the 'Spirit of adoption' (v. 15), the Spirit that maketh intercession for us (v. 26). All other ways of mortification are vain; all helps leave us helpless; it must be done by the Spirit. Men, as the apostle intimates (Rom. 9:30-32), may attempt this work on other principles, by means and advantages administered on other accounts, as they always have done and do: but (saith he) this is the work of the Spirit; by him alone it is to be wrought, and by no other power is it to be brought about. Mortification from a self-strength, carried on by ways of self-invention, unto the end of a

self-righteousness, is the soul and substance of all false religion in the world: and this is a second principle of my ensuing discourse.

(4) *The duty itself*, 'mortify the deeds of the body', is next to be remarked.

Three things are here to be inquired into: (i) What is meant by 'the body'; (ii) What by 'the deeds of the body'; (iii) What by 'mortifying' them.

(i) The body, in the close of the verse, is the same with the flesh, in the beginning; 'if ye live after the flesh, ye shall die', but if ye 'mortify the deeds of the body', that is, of the flesh. It is that which the apostle hath all along discoursed of, under the name of the flesh: which is evident from the prosecution of the contrast between the Spirit and the flesh, before and after. The body, then, is here taken for that corruption and pravity of our natures, whereof the body in a great part is the seat and instrument; the very members of the body being made servants unto unrighteousness thereby (Rom. 6:19). It is indwelling sin, the corrupted flesh or lust, that is intended. Many reasons might be given for this figurative expression, that I shall not now insist on. The body here is the same with the 'old man', and the 'body of sin' (Rom. 6:6); or it may, by another figure, express the whole person, considered as corrupted, and the seat of lusts and distempered affections.

(ii) The deeds of the body. The word 'deeds' denoteth, indeed, the outward actions chiefly, 'the works of the flesh', as they are called (Gal. 5:19), which are there said to be manifest, and are enumerated. Now, though the outward deeds are here only expressed, yet the inward and nearest causes are chiefly intended. The 'axe is to be laid to the root of the tree': the deeds of the flesh are to be mortified in their causes, from whence they spring. The apostle calls them deeds, as that which every lust tends unto: though it do but conceive, and prove abortive, it aims to bring forth a perfect sin.

Having, both in the seventh and the beginning of this chapter, treated of indwelling lust and sin as the fountain and principle of all sinful actions, he here mentions its destruction, under the name of the effects which it doth produce. 'The deeds of the body', are as much as 'the wisdom of the flesh' (Rom. 8:6), by a figure of the same nature with the former; or as the 'passions and lusts of the flesh' (Gal. 5:24), whence the deeds and fruits of it do arise: and in this sense is 'the body' used (v. 10); 'the body is dead because of sin'.

(iii) To mortify; or, as in the original, 'if ye put to death'; a metaphorical expression, taken from the putting of any living thing to death. To kill a man, or any other living thing, is to take away the principle of all his strength, vigour and power, so that he cannot act, or exert, or put forth any proper actings of his own. So it is in this case. Indwelling sin is compared to a person, a living person, called the old man, with his faculties and properties, his wisdom, craft, subtlety, strength; this (says the apostle) must be killed, put to death, mortified; that is, have its power, life, vigour and strength to produce its effects, taken away by the Spirit. It is indeed meritoriously, and by way of example, utterly mortified and slain by the cross of Christ; and the old man is thence said to be 'crucified with Christ' (Rom. 6:6), and 'ourselves to be dead with him' (v. 8), and really, initially in regeneration (Rom. 6:3-5), when a principle contrary to it, and *destructive* of it (Gal. 5:17), is planted in our hearts. But the whole work is by degrees to be carried on towards perfection all our days. Of this, more in the process of our discourse.

The intention of the apostle in this prescription of the duty mentioned, is, that the mortification of indwelling sin, remaining in our mortal bodies, in order that it may not have life and power to bring forth the works or deeds of the flesh, is the constant duty of believers.

(5) *The promise unto this duty is life*; 'ye shall live'. The life promised is opposed to the death threatened in the clause foregoing, 'if ye live after the flesh, ye shall die'; which the same apostle elsewhere expresseth: 'ye shall of the flesh reap corruption' (Gal. 5:8), or destruction from God. Now, perhaps, the word may not only intend eternal life, but also the spiritual life in Christ which here we have; not as to the essence and being of it, which is already enjoyed by believers; but as to the joy, comfort and vigour of it: as the apostle says in another case, 'Now I live, if ye stand fast' (1 Thess. 3:8), now my life will do me good, I shall have joy and

comfort with my life. 'Ye shall live'; lead a good, vigorous, comfortable, spiritual life whilst you are here, and obtain eternal life hereafter.

Supposing what was said before, of the connection between mortification and eternal life, as of means and end, I shall add only, as a second motive to the duty prescribed, that, *the vigour, and power, and comfort of our spiritual life depend on the mortification of the deeds of the flesh.*

CHAPTER 2

The principal assertion concerning the necessity of mortification proposed to confirmation. Mortification the duty of the best believers (Col. 3:5; 1 Cor. 9:27). Indwelling sin always abides: no perfection in this life (Phil. 3:12; 1 Cor. 13:12; 2 Pet. 3:18; Gal. 5:17, etc). The activity of abiding sin in believers (Rom. 7:23; Jas. 4:5; Heb. 12:1). Its fruitfulness and tendency. Every lust aims at the height in its kind. The Spirit and new nature given to contend against indwelling sin (Gal. 5:17; 2 Pet. 1:4, 5; Rom. 7:23). The fearful issue of the neglect of mortification (Rev. 3:2; Heb. 3:13). The first general principle of the whole discourse hence confirmed. Want of this duty lamented.

Having laid this foundation, a brief confirmation of the forementioned principal deductions will lead me to what I chiefly intend.

The first is, that the choicest believers, who are assuredly freed from the condemning power of sin, ought yet to make it their business, all their days, to mortify the indwelling power of sin.

So the apostle: 'Mortify therefore your members which are upon the earth' (Col. 3:5). Whom speaks he to? Such as were risen with Christ (v. 1); such as were dead with him (v. 3); such as whose life Christ was, and who should appear with him in glory (v. 4). Do you mortify; do you make it your daily work; be always at it whilst you live; cease not a day from this work; be killing sin, or it will be killing you. Your being dead with Christ virtually, your being quickened with him, will not excuse you from this work. And our Saviour tells us how his Father deals with every branch in him that beareth fruit, every true and living branch; 'he purgeth it, that it may bring forth more fruit' (John 15:2). He prunes it, and that not for a day or two, but whilst it is a branch in this world. And the apostle tells you what was his practice: 'I keep under my body and bring it into subjection' (1 Cor. 9:27). I do it (saith he) daily; it is the work of my life; I omit it not; this is my business. And if this were the work and business of Paul, who was so incomparably exalted in grace, light, revelations, enjoyments, privileges, consolations, above the ordinary measure of believers, where may we possibly bottom an exemption from this work and duty whilst we are in this world? Some brief accounts of the reasons hereof may be given.

(1) Indwelling sin always abides whilst we are in this world; therefore it is always to be mortified. The vain, foolish and ignorant disputes of men about perfect keeping of the commands of God, of perfection in this

life, of being wholly and perfectly dead to sin, I now meddle not with. It is more than probable that the men of those abominations never knew what belonged to the keeping of any one of God's commands, and are so much below perfection of degrees that they never attained to a perfection of parts in obedience, or universal obedience in sincerity. And therefore many in our days who have talked of perfection, have been wiser, and have affirmed it to consist in knowing no difference between good and evil. Not that they are perfect in the things we call good, but that all is alike to them; and the height of wickedness is their perfection. Others, who have found out a new way to it, by denying original indwelling sin, and tempering the spirituality of the law of God unto men's carnal hearts, as they have sufficiently discovered themselves to be ignorant of the life of Christ and the power of it in believers, so they have invented a new righteousness that the gospel knows not of, being vainly puffed up by their fleshly minds.

As for us, who dare not be wise above what is written, nor boast, by other men's lines, of what God hath not done for us, we say, that indwelling sin lives in us in some measure and degree whilst we are in this world. We dare not speak 'as though we had already attained, or were already perfect' (Phil. 3:12); our 'inward man is to be renewed day by day' whilst here we live (2 Cor. 4:16): and according to the renovations of the new, are the breaches and decays of the old. While we are here, we 'know but in part' (1 Cor.

13:12): having a remaining darkness to be gradually removed by our 'growth in the knowledge of our Lord Jesus Christ' (2 Pet. 3:18). And the flesh lusteth against the Spirit, so that we cannot do the things that we would, and are therefore defective in our obedience as well as in our light (Gal. 5:17; 1 John 1:8). We have a 'body of death' (Rom. 7:24), from whence we are not delivered but by the 'death of our bodies' (Phil. 3:21). Now it being our duty to mortify, to be killing sin, whilst it is in us we must be at work. He that is appointed to kill an enemy, if he leave striking before the other ceases living, doth but half his work (Gal. 6:9; Heb. 12:1; 2 Cor. 7:1).

(2) Sin doth not only still abide in us, but is still acting, still labouring to bring forth the deeds of the flesh. When sin lets us alone, we may let sin alone: but as sin is never less quiet than when it seems to be most quiet, and its waters are for the most part deep when they are still, so ought our contrivances against it to be vigorous at all times, in all conditions, even where there is least suspicion.

Sin doth not only abide in us, but the 'law of the members' is still 'rebelling against the law of the mind' (Rom. 7:23), and 'the spirit that dwells in us lusteth to envy' (Jas. 4:5). It is always in continual work, 'the flesh lusteth against the Spirit' (Gal. 5:17). Lust is still tempting, and conceiving sin (Jas. 1:14). In every moral action, it is always either inclining to evil, or hindering from that which is good, or unframing the spirit from communion with God. It inclines to evil: 'the evil that I would not, that I do', saith the apostle (Rom. 7:19). Whence is that? Why, because 'in me, that is, in my flesh, dwelleth no good thing'. And it hinders from good: 'the good that I would do, that I do not' (v. 19). Upon the same account, either I do it not, or not as I should; all my holy things being defiled by this sin. 'The flesh lusteth against the Spirit, that ye cannot do the things that ye would' (Gal. 5:17). And it unframes our spirit, and thence is called 'the sin that so easily besets us' (Heb. 12:1); on which account are those grievous complaints that the apostle makes of it (Rom. 7). So that sin is always acting, always conceiving, always seducing and tempting.

Who can say that he had ever any thing to do with God, or for God, that indwelling sin had not a hand in the corrupting of what he did? And this trade will it drive, more or less, all our days. If, then, sin will be always acting, and we be not always mortifying, we are lost creatures. He that stands still, and suffers his enemies to double blows upon him without resistance, will undoubtedly be conquered in the issue. If sin be subtle, watchful, strong and always at work in the business of killing our souls, and we be slothful, negligent, foolish, in proceeding to the ruin thereof, can we expect a comfortable event? There is not a day but sin foils or is foiled, prevails or is prevailed on; and it will be so, whilst we live in this world. I shall discharge him from this duty who can bring sin to a composition, to a cessation of arms in this warfare: if it will spare him any one day, in any one duty (provided he be a person that is acquainted with the spirituality of obedience, and the subtlety of sin), let him say to his soul, as to this duty, 'Soul, take thy rest.' The saints whose souls breathe after deliverance from its perplexing rebellion, know there is no safety against it but in a constant warfare.

(3) Sin will not only be striving, acting, rebelling, troubling, disquieting; but, if let alone, if not continually mortified, it will bring forth great, cursed, scandalous, soul-destroying sins. The apostle tells us what the works and fruits of it are: 'The works of the flesh are manifest, which are these: Adultery, fornication, uncleanness, lasciviousness, idolatry, witchcraft, hatred, variance, emulations, wrath, strife, seditions, heresies, envyings, murders, drunkenness, revellings, and such like' (Gal. 5:19-21). You know what it did in David, and sundry others.

Sin aims always at the utmost: every time it rises up to tempt or entice, might it have its own course, it would go out to the utmost sin of that kind. Every unclean thought or glance would be adultery, if it could; every covetous desire would be oppression; every thought of unbelief would be atheism, might it grow to its head. Men may come to that, that sin may not be heard speaking a scandalous word in their hearts; that is, provoking to any great sin with scandal in its mouth: but every rise of lust, might it have its course, would come to the height of villainy. It is like the grave, that is never satisfied. And herein lies no small share of the deceitfulness of sin, by which it prevails to the hardening of men, and so to their ruin (Heb. 3:13). It is modest, as it were, in its first motions and proposals; but having once got footing in the heart by them, it constantly makes good its ground, and presseth on to some further degrees in the same kind.

This new acting and pressing forward, makes the soul take little notice of what an entrance is already made to a falling off from God. It thinks all is indifferent well, if there be no further progress. And so far as the soul is made insensible to any sin, that is, as to such a sense as the gospel requireth, so far it is hardened. But sin is still pressing forward: and that because it hath no bounds but utter relinquishment of God, and opposition to him. That it proceeds towards its height by degrees, making good the ground it hath got by hardness, is not from its nature, but its deceitfulness.

Now nothing can prevent this, but mortification. That withers the root and strikes at the head of sin every hour, so that it is crossed in whatever it aims at. There is not the best saint in the world but, if he should give over this duty, would fall into as many cursed sins as ever any did of his kind.

(4) This is one main reason why the Spirit and the new nature are given unto us, that we may have a principle within whereby to oppose sin and lust. 'The flesh lusteth against the Spirit.' Well, and what then? Why, 'the Spirit also lusteth against the flesh' (Gal. 5:17).

There is a propensity in the Spirit, or spiritual new nature, to be acting against the flesh, as well as in the flesh to be acting against the Spirit. So 2 Peter 1:4, 5; it is our 'participation of the Divine nature' that gives us an 'escape from the pollutions that are in the world through lust'; and there is a law of the mind as well as a law of the members (Rom. 7:23). Now this is, first, the most unjust and unreasonable thing in the world; when two combatants are engaged, to bind one and keep him up from doing his utmost, and to leave the other at liberty to wound him at his pleasure: and, second, the foolishest thing in the world to bind him who fights for our eternal condition, and to let him alone who seeks and violently attempts our everlasting ruin. The contest is for our lives and souls. Not to be daily employing the Spirit and new nature for the mortifying of sin, is to neglect that excellent succour which God hath given us against our greatest enemy. If we neglect to make use of what we have received, God may justly hold his hand from giving us more. His graces, as well as his gifts, are bestowed on us to use, exercise and trade with. Not to be daily mortifying sin is to sin against the goodness, kindness, wisdom, grace and love of God, who hath furnished us with a principle of doing it.

(5) Negligence in this duty casts the soul into a perfectly contrary condition to that which the apostle affirms was his; 'though our outward man perish, our inward man is renewed day by day' (2 Cor. 4:16). In

these, the inward man perisheth, and the outward man is renewed day by day. Sin is as the house of David, and grace as the house of Saul. Exercise and success are the two main cherishers of grace in the heart: when it is suffered to lie still, it withers and decays; the things of it are ready to die, and sin gets ground towards the hardening of the heart (Rev. 3:2; Heb. 3:13). This is that which I intend: by the omission of this duty, grace withers, lust flourisheth, and the frame of the heart grows worse and worse: and the Lord knows what desperate and fearful issues it hath had with many.

Where sin, through the neglect of mortification, gets a considerable victory, it breaks the bones of the soul (Ps. 31:10; 51:8); and makes a man weak, sick and ready to die (Ps. 38:3-5), so that he cannot look up (Ps. 40:12; Isa. 33:24). And when poor creatures will take blow after blow, wound after wound, foil after foil, and never rouse up themselves to a vigorous opposition, can they expect any thing but to be hardened through the deceitfulness of sin, and that their souls should bleed to death (2 John 8)? Indeed, it is a sad thing to consider the fearful issues of this neglect, which lie under our eyes every day. See we not those, whom we knew as humble, melting, broken-hearted Christians, tender and fearful to offend, zealous for God, and all his ways, his sabbaths and ordinances, grown, through a neglect of watching unto this duty, earthly, carnal, cold, wrathful, complying with the men of the world and things of the world, to the scandal of religion, and the fearful temptation of them that know them? The truth is, what between placing mortification in a rigid, stubborn frame of spirit, which is, for the most part, earthly, legal, censorious, partial, consistent with wrath, envy, malice, pride on the one hand, and pretences of liberty, grace, and I know not what on the other, true evangelical mortification is almost lost amongst us: of which afterwards.

(6) It is our duty to be perfecting holiness in the fear of the Lord (2 Cor. 7:1); to be growing in grace every day (1 Pet. 2:2; 2 Pet. 3:18); to be renewing our inward man day by day (2 Cor. 4:16). Now, this cannot be done without the daily mortifying of sin: sin sets its strength against every act of holiness, and against every degree we grow to. Let not that man think he makes any progress in holiness, who walks not over the neck of his lusts. He, who doth not kill sin in his way, takes no steps towards his journey's end. He, who finds not opposition from it, and who sets not himself in every particular to its mortification, is at peace with it, not dying to it.

This, then, is the first general principle of our ensuing discourse. Notwithstanding the meritorious mortification, if I may so speak, of all and every sin in the cross of Christ; notwithstanding the real foundation of universal mortification laid in our first conversion, by conviction of sin, humiliation for sin, and the implantation of a new principle, opposite to it, and destructive of it; yet sin doth so remain, so act and work in the best of believers whilst they live in this world, that the constant daily mortification of it is all their days incumbent on them.

Before I proceed to the consideration of the next principle, I cannot but complain, by the way, of many professors of these days; who, instead of bringing forth such great and evident fruits of mortification as are expected, scarce bear any leaves of it. There is, indeed, a bright light fallen upon the men of this generation, and together therewith many spiritual gifts communicated; which, with some other considerations, have wonderfully enlarged the bounds of professors and profession; both they and it are exceedingly multiplied and increased. Hence, there is noise of religion and religious duties in every corner: preaching in abundance; and that not in an empty, light, trivial and vain manner, as formerly, but in a good proportion of a spiritual gift: so that if you will measure the number of believers by light, gifts and profession, the church may have cause to say, 'Who hath borne me all these?'.

But now, if you will take the measure of them by this great discriminating grace of Christians, perhaps you will find their number not so multiplied. Where, almost, is that professor who owes his conversion to these days of light, and so talks and professes at such a rate of spirituality as few in former days were in any measure acquainted with (I will not judge them, but), perhaps boasting what the Lord hath done in them – that doth not give evidence of a miserably unmortified heart? If vain spending of time, idleness, unprofitableness in men's places, envy, strife, variance, emulations, wrath, pride, worldliness, selfishness, be badges of Christians, we have them on us and amongst us in abundance. And if it be so with them who have so much light, and which we hope is saving, what shall we say of some who would be accounted religious, and yet despise gospel light, and as for the duty we have in hand know no more of it than what consists in men's denying themselves sometimes in outward enjoyments, which is one of the outmost branches of it and which yet they will seldom practise? The good Lord sends out a spirit of mortification to cure our distempers, or we are in a sad condition.

There are two evils which certainly attend every unmortified professor: the first in himself, and the other in respect of others.

(1) In himself. Let him pretend what he will, he hath slight thoughts of sin: at least of sins of daily infirmity. The root of an unmortified course is the digestion of sin, without bitterness in the heart. When a man hath fixed his imagination to such an apprehension of grace and mercy, as to be able without bitterness to swallow and digest daily sins, that man is at the very brink of turning the grace of God into lasciviousness, and being hardened by the deceitfulness of sin. Neither is there a greater evidence in the world of a false and rotten heart, than to drive such a trade. To use, for the countenancing of sin, the blood of Christ, which is given to cleanse us (1 John 1:7; Titus 2:14); the exaltation of Christ, which is to give us

repentance (Acts 5:31); the doctrine of grace, which teaches us to deny all ungodliness (Titus 2:11, 12); is a rebellion, that, in the issue, will break the bones. At this door have gone out from us most of the professors that have apostatized in the days wherein we live. For a while they were most of them under convictions; these kept them unto duties, and brought them to profession. So they 'escaped the pollutions that are in the world, through the knowledge of our Lord Jesus Christ' (2 Pet. 2:20). But having got an acquaintance with the doctrine of the gospel, and being weary of duty for which they had no principle, they began, from the doctrine of grace, to countenance themselves in manifold neglects. Now when once this evil had laid hold of them, they speedily tumbled into perdition.

(2) Upon others it hath an evil influence, on a two-fold account.

(i) It hardens them by begetting in them a persuasion that they are in as good condition as the best professors. Whatever they see in them is so stained, for want of this mortification, that it is of no value with them. They have zeal for religion; but it is accompanied with want of forbearance and universal righteousness. They deny prodigality, but with worldliness: they separate from the world, but live wholly to themselves, taking no care to exercise loving-kindness in the earth. Or they talk spiritually, and live vainly; mention communion with God, and are every way conformed to the world; boasting of forgiveness of sin, and never forgiving others: and with such considerations do poor creatures harden their hearts in their unregeneracy.

(ii) They deceive them, in making them believe that if they can come up to their condition it shall be well with them. And so it grows an ordinary thing to have the great temptation of repute in religion to wrestle withal: when they may go far beyond them, as to what appears in them, and yet come short of eternal life. But of these things, and all the evils of unmortified walking, afterwards.

CHAPTER 3

The second general principle of the means of mortification proposed to confirmation. The Spirit the only author of this work. Vanity of popish mortification discovered. Many means of it used by them not appointed by God. Those appointed by him abused. The mistakes of others in this business. The Spirit is promised believers for this work (Ezek. 11:19; 36:26). All that we receive from Christ is by the Spirit. How the Spirit mortifies sin (Gal. 5:19-23). The several ways of his operations to this end proposed. How his work, and our duty.

The next principle relates to the great sovereign cause of the mortification treated of, which, in the words laid for the foundation of this discourse, is said to be the Spirit, that is, the Holy Ghost, as was evinced.

He only is sufficient for this work. All ways and means without him are as a thing of nought; and he is the great efficient of it; he 'works in us as he pleases'.

(1) In vain do men seek other remedies; they shall not be healed by them. What several ways have been prescribed for this, to have sin mortified, is known. The greatest part of popish religion, of that which looks most like religion in their profession, consists in mistaken ways and means of mortification. This is the pretence of their 'rough garments', whereby they deceive. Their vows, orders, fastings, penances, are all built on this ground; they are all for the mortifying of sin. Their preachings, sermons and books of devotion look all this way. Hence those who interpret the 'locusts' that came out of the 'bottomless pit' (Rev. 9:2) to be the friars of the Romish church, who are said to torment men so that 'they should seek death and not find it' (v. 6), think that they did it by their stinging sermons, whereby they convinced them of sin, but being not able to discover the remedy for the healing and mortifying of it, they kept them in such perpetual anguish and terror, and such trouble in their consciences, that they 'desired to die'. This, I say, is the substance and glory of their religion. But what with their labouring to mortify dead creatures, ignorant of the nature and end of the work; what with the poison they mixed with it, in their persuasion of its merit, yea, supererogation, as they style their unnecessary merit, with a proud and barbarous title; their glory is their shame. But of them and their mortification, more afterwards (ch. 8).

That the ways and means to be used for the mortification of sin, invented by them, are still insisted on and prescribed for the same end by some who should have more light and knowledge of the gospel, is known. Such directions to this purpose have of late been given by some, and are greedily catched at by others, professing themselves Protestants, as might have become popish devotionists three or four hundred years ago. Such outside endeavours, such bodily exercises, such self-performances, such merely legal duties, without the least mention of Christ or his Spirit, are varnished over with swelling words of vanity as the only means and expedients for the mortification of sin, so as to discover a deep-rooted unacquaintedness with the power of God and mystery of the gospel. The considering hereof was one motive to the publishing of this plain discourse.

Now, the reasons why the Papists can never, with all their endeavours, truly mortify any one sin, are these, amongst others.

(i) Because many of the ways and means they use and insist upon for this end were never appointed of God for that purpose. Now there is nothing in religion that hath any efficacy for compassing an end, but it hath it from God's appointment of it to that purpose. Such as these are, their rough garments, their vows, penances, disciplines, their course of monastical life and the like, concerning all of them God will say 'Who hath required these things at your hands?' and, 'In vain do you worship me, teaching for doctrines the traditions of men'. Of the same nature are sundry self-vexations, insisted on by others.

(ii) Because those things that are appointed of God as means are not used by them in their due place and order; such as praying, fasting, watching, meditation and the like: these have their use in the business in hand. But whereas they are all to be looked on as streams, they look on them as the fountain. Whereas they affect and accomplish the end only as means subordinate to the Spirit and faith, they look to them to do it by virtue of the work wrought. If they fast so much, and pray so much, and keep their hours and times, the work is done. As the apostle says of some in another case, 'they are always learning, never coming to the knowledge of the truth'; so, they are always mortifying, but never come to any sound mortification. In a word, they have sundry means to mortify the natural man as to the natural life we here lead: none to mortify lust or corruption.

This is the general mistake of men, ignorant of the gospel, about this thing; and it lies at the bottom of very much of that superstition and will-worship that hath been brought into the world. What horrible self-macerations were practised by some of the ancient authors of monastical devotion! What violence did they offer to nature! What extremity of sufferings did they put themselves upon! Search their ways and principles to the bottom, and you will find that they had no other root but this mistake: namely, that attempting rigid mortification, they fell upon the natural man instead of the corrupt old man; upon the body wherein we live, instead of the body of death.

Neither will the natural popery that is in others do it. Men are galled with the guilt of a sin that hath prevailed over them; they instantly promise to themselves and God that they will do so no more; they watch over themselves and pray for a season, until this heat waxes cold and the sense of sin is worn off; and so mortification goes also, and sin returns to its former dominion. Duties are excellent food for a healthy soul; they are no physic for a sick soul. He that turns his meat into his medicine, must expect no great operation. Spiritually sick men cannot sweat out their distemper with working. But this is the way of men who deceive their own souls; as we shall see afterwards.

That none of these ways are sufficient is evident from the nature of the work itself that is to be done; it is a work that requires so many concurrent actings in it, as no self-endeavour can reach unto; and is of such a kind that an almighty energy is necessary for its accomplishment, as shall be afterwards manifested.

(2) It is, then, the work of the Spirit. For,

(i) He is promised of God to be given to us, to do this work. The taking away of the stony heart, that is, the stubborn, proud, rebellious, unbelieving heart is, in general, the work of mortification that we treat of. Now this is still promised to be done by the Spirit, 'I will give my Spirit, and take away the stony heart' (Ezek. 11:19; 36:26); and by the Spirit of God is this work wrought, when all means fail (Isa. 57:17, 18).

(ii) We have all our mortification from the gift of Christ, and all the gifts of Christ are communicated to us, and given us, by the Spirit of Christ. 'Without Christ we can do nothing' (John 15:5). All communications of supplies and relief, in the beginnings, increasings, actings of any grace whatever from him, are by the Spirit, by whom he alone works in and upon believers. From him we have our mortification. 'He is exalted, and made a Prince and a Saviour, to give repentance unto us' (Acts 5:31); and of our repentance our mortification is no small portion. How doth he do it? Having received the promise of the Holy Ghost, he sends him abroad for that end (Acts 2:33). You know the manifold promises he made of sending the Spirit, as Tertullian speaks, to do the works that he had to accomplish in us.

The resolution of one or two questions will now lead me nearer to what I principally intend.

The first is:

Question: How doth the Spirit mortify sin?

Answer: In general, three ways.

(1) By causing our hearts to abound in grace, and the fruits that are contrary to the flesh and the fruits thereof, and to the principles of them. So the apostle opposes the fruits of the flesh and of the Spirit: the fruits of the flesh, says he, are so and so (Gal. 5:19, 20); but, says he, the fruits of the Spirit are quite contrary, quite of another sort (vv. 22, 23). Yea, but what if these are in us and do abound; may not the other abound also? No, says he (v. 24); 'they that are Christ's have crucified the flesh, with the affections and lusts'. But how? Why by 'living in the Spirit, and walking after the Spirit' (v. 25); that is, by the abounding of these graces of the Spirit in us, and walking according to them. For, saith the apostle, 'these are contrary one to another' (v. 17), so that they cannot

both be in the same subject, in any intense or high degree. This renewing of us by the Holy Ghost, as it is called (Titus 3:5), is one great way of mortification: he causes us to grow, thrive, flourish and abound in those graces which are contrary, opposite, and destructive to all the fruits of the flesh, and to the quiet or thriving of indwelling sin itself.

(2) By a real, physical efficiency on the root and habit of sin, for the weakening, destroying and taking it away. Hence he is called a 'Spirit of judgment and burning' (Isa. 4:4), really consuming and destroying our lusts. He takes away the stony heart by an almighty efficiency; for as he begins the work as to its kind, so he carries it on as to its degrees. He is the fire which burns up the very root of lust.

(3) He brings the cross of Christ into the heart of a sinner by faith, and gives us communion with Christ in his death, and fellowship in his sufferings; of the manner whereof more afterwards.

The second is,

Question: If this be the work of the Spirit alone, how is it that we are exhorted to it? Seeing the Spirit of God only can do it, let the work be left wholly to him.

Answer: 1. It is no otherwise the work of the Spirit, than as all graces and good works which are in us are his. He works in us 'to will and to do of his own good pleasure' (Phil. 2:13); 'He works all our works in us' (Isa. 26:12); 'The work of faith with power' (2 Thess. 1:11; Col. 2:12). He causes us to pray and is 'a Spirit of supplication' (Rom.

8:26; Zech. 12:10). And yet we are exhorted, and are to be exhorted, to all these.

Answer: 2. He doth not so work our mortification in us as not to keep it still an act of our obedience. The Holy Ghost works in us and upon us, as we are fit to be wrought in and upon; that is, so as to preserve our own liberty and free obedience. He works upon our understandings, wills, consciences and affections, agreeably to their own natures: he works in us and with us, not against us or without us: so that his assistance is an encouragement as to the facilitating of the work, and no occasion of neglect as to the work itself. And indeed, I might here bewail the endless foolish labour of poor souls who, being convinced of sin and not able to stand against the power of their convictions, do set themselves by innumerable perplexing ways and duties to keep down sin: but, being strangers to the Spirit of God, all in vain. They combat without victory, have war without peace, and are in slavery all their days. They spend their strength for that which is not bread, and their labour for that which profiteth not.

This is the saddest warfare that any poor creature can be engaged in. A soul under the power of conviction from the law, is pressed to fight against sin, but hath no strength for the combat. They cannot but fight, and they can never conquer; they are like men thrust on the sword of enemies, in purpose to be slain. The law drives them on, and sin beats them back. Sometimes they think indeed that they have foiled sin, when they have only raised a dust so that they see it not; that is, they distemper their natural affections of fear, sorrow and anguish, which makes them believe that sin is conquered, when it is not touched. But that time they are cold, they must to the battle again; and the lust which they thought to be slain, appears to have had no wound.

And if the case be so sad with them who labour and strive, and yet enter not into the kingdom, what is their condition who despise all this; who are perpetually under the power and dominion of sin, and love to have it so; and are troubled at nothing but that they cannot make sufficient provision for the flesh, to fulfil the lusts thereof?

CHAPTER 4

The last principle: Of the usefulness of mortification.
The vigour and comfort of our spiritual life depend on
our mortification. In what sense? Not absolutely and
necessarily. Heman's condition (Ps. 88). Not as the next
and immediate cause. As a means, by removing the
contrary. The desperate effects of unmortified lust; it
weakens the soul sundry ways (Ps. 88:3, 8), and darkens
it. All graces improved by the mortification of sin. The
best evidence of sincerity.

The last principle I shall insist on, omitting the necessity of mortification unto life, and the certainty of life upon mortification, is that the life, vigour and comfort of our spiritual life depend much on our mortification of sin.

Strength, and comfort, and power, and peace in our walking with God are the things of our desires. Were any of us asked seriously, what it is that troubles us, we must refer it to one of these heads; either we want strength, or power, vigour, and life, in our obedience, in our walking with God; or we want peace, comfort and consolation therein. Whatever it is that may befall a believer which doth not belong to one of these two heads, deserves not to be mentioned in the days of our complaints. Now all these do much depend on a constant course of mortification; concerning which observe:

(1) I do not say they proceed from it, as though they were necessarily tied to it. A man may be carried on in a constant course of mortification all his days, and yet perhaps never enjoy a good day of peace and consolation. So it was with Heman (Ps. 88). His life was a life of perpetual mortification and walking with God; yet terrors and wounds were his portion all his days. But God singled out Heman, a choice friend, to make him an example to them that afterwards should be in distress. Canst thou complain if it be no otherwise with thee than it was with Heman, that eminent servant of God? and this shall be his praise to the end of the world. God makes it his prerogative to speak peace and consolation (Isa. 57:18, 19). I will do that work, says God; I will comfort him (v. 18). But how? By an immediate work of the new creation: 'I create it,' says God. The use of means for the obtaining of peace is ours; the bestowing of it is God's prerogative.

(2) In the ways instituted by God for giving us life, vigour, courage and consolation, mortification is not one of the immediate causes of it. It is the privilege of our adoption, made known to our souls, that gives us immediately these things. The Spirit's 'bearing witness

with our spirits that we are the children of God'; his giving us 'a new name', and 'a white stone', adoption and justification, that is, as to the sense and knowledge of them; these are the immediate causes, in the hand of the Spirit, of these things. But this I say,

(3) In our ordinary walking with God, and in an ordinary course of his dealing with us, the vigour and comfort of our spiritual lives depend much on our mortification, not only as an indispensable requisite, but as a thing that hath an effectual influence thereunto. For,

(i) This alone keeps sin from depriving us of the one and the other. Every unmortified sin will certainly do two things; first, it will weaken the soul, and deprive it of its vigour; secondly, it will darken the soul, and deprive it of its comfort and peace.

[a] It weakens the soul, and deprives it of its strength. When David had for a while harboured an unmortified lust in his heart, it broke all his bones, and left him no spiritual strength; hence he complained that he was sick, weak, wounded, faint. 'There is,' saith he, 'no soundness in me' (Ps. 38:3); 'I am feeble and sore broken' (v. 8); 'yea, I cannot so much as look up' (Ps. 40:12). An unmortified lust will drink up the spirit and all the vigour of the soul, and weaken it for all duties.

For, first of all, it untunes and unframes the heart itself, by entangling its affections. It diverts the heart from that spiritual frame that is required for vigorous communion with God. It lays hold on the affections, rendering its object beloved and desirable, and so

51

expelling the love of the Father (1 John 2:15; 3:17). So that the soul cannot say uprightly and truly to God, 'Thou art my portion', having something else that it loves. Fear, desire, hope, which are the choice affections of the soul, that should be full of God, will be one way or other entangled with it.

Again, it fills the thoughts with contrivances about it. Thoughts are the great purveyors of the soul, to bring in provision to satisfy its affections; and if sin remain unmortified in the heart, they must ever and anon be making provision for the flesh, to fulfil the lusts thereof. They must glaze, adorn and dress the objects of the flesh, and bring them home to give satisfaction. And this they are able to do, in the service of a defiled imagination, beyond all expression.

Further, it breaks out, and actually hinders duty. The ambitious man must be studying, and the worldling must be working or contriving, and the sensual vain person providing himself for vanity, when they should be engaged in the worship of God.

Were this my present business, to set forth the breaches, ruin, weakness, desolation, that one unmortified lust will bring upon a soul, this discourse must be extended much beyond my intention.

[b] As sin weakens, so it darkens the soul. It is a cloud, a thick cloud, that spreads itself over the face of the soul, and intercepts all the beams of God's love and favour. It takes away all sense of the privilege of our adoption; and if the soul begins to gather up thoughts of consolation, sin quickly scatters them. Of which afterwards.

Now in this respect do the vigour and power of our spiritual life depend on our mortification. It is the only means of the removal of that which will allow us neither the one nor the other. Men that are sick and wounded under the power of lust, make many applications for help; they cry to God, when the perplexity of their thoughts overwhelms them; even to God do they cry, but are not delivered; in vain do they use many remedies, they shall not be healed. So Hosea 5:13: 'Ephraim saw his sickness, and Judah his wound', and attempted sundry remedies; nothing will do, until they come (v. 15) to acknowledge their offence. Men may see their sickness and wounds, but yet if they make not due applications, their cure will not be effected.

(ii) Mortification prunes all the graces of God, and makes room for them in our hearts to grow. The life and vigour of our spiritual lives consist in the vigour and flourishing of the plants of grace in our hearts. Now, as you may see in a garden, let there be a precious herb planted, and let the ground be untilled, and weeds grow about it; perhaps it will live still, but be a poor, withering, unuseful thing. You must look and search for it, and sometimes you can scarce find it; and when you do, you can scarce know it, whether it be the plant you look for or no: and suppose it be, you can make no use of it at all. Whereas, let another of the same kind be set in ground naturally as barren and bad as the other, but let it be well weeded and every thing that is noxious and hurtful removed from it, it flourishes and thrives; you may see it at first look into the garden, and have it for your use when you please. So it is with the graces of the Spirit that are planted in our hearts. That is true, that they are still, they abide, in a heart where there is some neglect of mortification; but they are ready to die (Rev. 3:2), they are withering and decaying. The heart is like the sluggard's field, so overgrown with weeds that you can scarce see the good corn. Such a man may search for faith, love and zeal, and scarce be able to find any; and if he do discover that these graces are there, still alive and sincere, yet they are so weak, so clogged with lusts, that they are of very little use; they remain indeed, but are ready to die. But now let the heart be cleansed by mortification; the weeds of lust constantly and daily rooted up, as they spring daily, nature being their proper soil; let room be made for grace to thrive and flourish; how will every grace act its part, and be ready for every use and purpose!

(iii) With regard to our peace, as there is nothing that hath any evidence of sincerity without mortification, so I know nothing that hath such an evidence of sincerity in it: which is no small foundation of our peace. Mortification is the soul's vigorous opposition to self; wherein sincerity is most evident.

CHAPTER 5

The principal intention of the whole discourse proposed. The first main case of conscience stated. What it is to mortify any sin, negatively considered. Not the utter destruction of it in this life. Not the dissimulation of it. Not the improvement of any natural principle. Not the diversion of it. Not an occasional conquest. Occasional conquests of sin, what, and when. Upon the eruption of sin in time of danger or trouble.

These things being premised, I come to my principal intention of handling some questions or practical cases that present themselves in this business of the mortification of sin in believers. The first, which is the head of all the rest and whereunto they are reduced, may be considered as lying under the ensuing proposal.

Suppose that a man is a true believer, and yet finds in himself a powerful indwelling sin, leading him captive to the law of it, consuming his heart with trouble, perplexing his thoughts, weakening his soul as to duties of communion with God, disquieting him as to peace, perhaps defiling his conscience and exposing him to hardening through the deceitfulness of sin. What shall he do? What course shall he take and insist on, for the mortification of this sin, lust, distemper or corruption, to such a degree as that, though it be not utterly destroyed, yet in his contest with it he may be enabled to keep up power, strength and peace, in communion with God?

In answer to this important inquiry, I shall do these things. First, show what it is to mortify any sin; and that both negatively and positively, that we be not mistaken in the foundation. Second, give general direction for such things as without which it will be utterly impossible for any one to get any sin truly and spiritually mortified. Third, draw out the particulars whereby this is to be done; in the whole carrying on this consideration, that it is not of the doctrine of mortification in general, but only in reference to the particular case before proposed, that I am treating.

First, Show what it is to mortify a sin.
(1) To mortify a sin is not utterly to kill it, root it out and destroy it, that it should have no more hold at all, nor residence in our hearts. It is true this is that which is aimed at, but this is not in this life to be accomplished. There is no man that truly sets himself to mortify any sin, but he aims at, intends, desires, its utter destruction, that it should leave neither root nor fruit in the heart or life. He would so kill it that it should never move or stir any more, cry or call, seduce or

tempt, to eternity. Its not being, is the thing aimed at.
Now, though doubtless there may be attained, by the
Spirit and grace of Christ, a wonderful success and
eminency of victory against any sin, so that a man may
have almost constant triumph over it; yet an utter
killing and destruction of it, that it should not be, is
not in this life to be expected. This Paul assures us of:
'not as though I had already attained, or were already
perfect' (Phil. 3:12). He was a choice saint, a pattern
for believers, one who, in faith and love and all the
fruits of the Spirit, had not his fellow in the world;
and on that account he ascribes perfection to himself
in comparison of others (v. 15). Yet he had not attained;
he was not perfect, but was following after. Still a vile
body he had, and we have, that must be changed by the
great power of Christ at last (v. 21). This we would have;
but God sees it best for us that we should be complete in
nothing in ourselves; that in all things we might be
complete in Christ, which is best for us (Col. 2:10).

(2) I think I need not say, it is not the dissimulation of
a sin. When a man, on some outward respects, forsakes
the practice of any sin, men perhaps may look on him
as a changed man; God knows that to his former
iniquity he hath added cursed hypocrisy, and is got into
a safer path to hell than he was in before. He hath got
another heart than he had, that is more cunning: not a
new heart, that is more holy.

(3) The mortification of sin consists not in the
improvement of a quiet, sedate nature. Some men have

an advantage by their natural constitution, so far as that they are not exposed to such violence of unruly passions and tumultuous affections as many others are. Let, now, these men cultivate and improve their natural frame and temper by discipline, consideration and prudence, and they may seem to themselves and others very mortified men, when perhaps their hearts are a standing sink of all abominations. One man, perhaps, is never so much troubled all his life with anger and passion, nor doth trouble others, as another is almost every day; and yet the latter may have done more to the mortification of the sin than the former. Let not such persons try their mortification by things to which their natural temper gives no life or vigour; let them bring themselves to self-denial, unbelief, envy or some such spiritual sin, and they will have a better view of themselves.

(4) A sin is not mortified when it is only diverted. Simon Magus for a season left his sorceries; but his covetousness and ambition, that set him on work, remained still, and would be acting another way. Therefore Peter tells him, 'I perceive thou art in the gall of bitterness' (Acts 8:23). Notwithstanding the profession thou hast made, notwithstanding thy relinquishment of thy sorceries, thy lust is as powerful as ever in thee; the same lust, only the streams of it are diverted; it now exerts and puts forth itself another way, but it is the old gall of bitterness still. A man may be sensible of a lust, set himself against the eruptions of it, take care that it shall not break forth as it hath

done; but in the mean time may suffer the same corrupted habit to vent itself some other way; as he who heals and skins a running sore thinks himself cured, but in the mean time his flesh festereth by the corruption of the same humour, and breaks out in another place. And this diversion, with the alterations that attend it, often befalls men on accounts wholly foreign unto grace. Change of the course of the life that a man was in, of relations, interests, designs, may affect it; yea, the very alterations in men's constitutions, occasioned by a natural progress in the course of their lives, may produce such changes as these. Men in age do not usually persist in the pursuit of youthful lusts, although they have never mortified any one of them. And the same is the case in bartering of lusts, and leaving to serve one that a man may serve another. He that changes pride for worldliness, sensuality for pharisaism, vanity in himself to the contempt of others: let him not think that he hath mortified the sin that he seems to have left. He hath changed his master, but is a servant still.

(5) Occasional conquests of sin do not amount to mortifying it. There are two occasions, or seasons, wherein a man who is contending with any sin, may seem to himself to have mortified it.

(i) When it hath had some sad eruption, to the disturbance of his peace, terror of his conscience, dread of scandal and evident provocation of God. This awakens and stirs up all that is in the man; it amazes him, fills him with abhorrency of sin and himself for it, sends him to God, makes him cry out as for life, abhor his lust as hell, and set himself against it. The whole man, spiritual and natural, being now awaked, sin shrinks in its head, appears not, but lies as dead before him. As when one hath drawn nigh to an army in the night, and hath killed a principal person: instantly the guards awake, men are roused up, and strict inquiry is made after the enemy, who, in the mean time, until the noise and tumult be over, hides himself, or lies like one that is dead, yet with firm resolution to do the like mischief again, upon the like opportunity. Upon the sin among the Corinthians, see how they muster up themselves for the surprisal and destruction of it (2 Cor. 7:11). So it is in a person, when a breach hath been made by his lust upon his conscience, quiet, perhaps credit, in some eruption of actual sin: carefulness, indignation, desire, fear, revenge, are all set on work about it and against it, and lust is quiet for a season, being run down before them: but when the hurry is over, and the inquest past, the thief appears again alive, and is as busy as ever at his work.

(ii) In a time of some judgment, calamity or pressing affliction, the heart is then taken up with thoughts and contrivances of flying from the present troubles, fears and dangers; this, as a convinced person concludes, is to be done only by relinquishment of sin, which gains peace with God. It is the anger of God in every affliction, that galls a convinced person. To be quit of this, men resolve at such times against their sins; sin shall never more have any place in them; they will never again give up themselves to the service of it. Accordingly, sin is quiet, stirs not, seems to be mortified. Not indeed that it hath received any one wound, but merely because the soul hath possessed its faculties, whereby sin should exert itself, with thoughts inconsistent with the motions thereof; which thoughts when they are laid aside, sin returns again to its former life and vigour. So they in Psalm 78:32-38, are a full instance and description of this frame of spirit whereof I speak.

> For all this they sinned still, and believed not for his wondrous works: therefore their days did he consume in vanity, and their years in trouble. When he slew them, then they sought him, and they returned, and inquired early after God. And they remembered that God was their rock, and the high God their redeemer. Nevertheless they did flatter him with their mouth, and they lied unto him with their tongues. For their heart was not right with him, neither were they stedfast in his covenant.

I no way doubt, but that when they sought and returned, and inquired early after God, they did it with full purpose of heart as to the relinquishment of their sins. That is expressed in the word 'returned'; to turn or return to the Lord, is by a relinquishment of sin. This they did early, with earnestness and diligence; but yet their sin was unmortified for all this (vv. 36, 37). And this is the state of many humiliations in the days of affliction; and a great deceit in the hearts of believers themselves lies oftentimes herein.

These and many other ways there are whereby poor souls deceive themselves, and suppose they have mortified their lusts, when they live and are mighty, and on every occasion break forth to their disturbance and disquietness.

CHAPTER 6

The mortification of sin in particular described. The several parts and degrees thereof. 1. The habitual weakening of its root and principle. The power of lust to tempt. Differences of that power to persons and times. 2. Constant fighting against sin. The parts thereof considered. 3. Success against it. The sum of this discourse.

What it is to mortify a sin in general, which will make farther way for particular directions, is next to be considered.

The mortification of a lust consists in three things.

1. *An habitual weakening of it.*

Every lust is a depraved habit or disposition, continually inclining the heart to evil: thence is that description of him who hath no lust truly mortified: 'Every imagination of the thoughts of his heart is only evil continually' (Gen. 6:5). He is always under the power of a strong bent and inclination to sin. And the reason why a natural man is not always, perpetually, in the

63

pursuit of some one lust, night and day, is because he hath many to serve, every one crying to be satisfied: thence he is carried on with great variety, but still in general he lies towards the satisfaction of self.

We will suppose, then, the lust or distemper, whose mortification is inquired after, to be in itself a strong, deeply-rooted, habitual inclination and bent of will and affections unto some actual sin (sin as to the matter of it, though not under that form as considered by the mind): always stirring up imaginations, thoughts and contrivances about the object of it. Hence men are said to have their hearts set upon evil; the bent of their spirits lies towards it, to make provision for the flesh (Rom. 13:4). And a sinful, depraved habit differs from all natural or moral habits whatever, as in many other things so in this, that whereas they incline the soul gently and suitably to itself, sinful habits impel with violence and impetuousness. Whence lusts are said 'to fight' or 'wage war against the soul' (1 Pet. 2:11); 'to rebel' or 'rise up in war', with that conduct and opposition which is usual therein (Rom. 7:23); 'to lead captive' or effectually to captivate upon success in battle; all works of great violence and impetuousness.

I might manifest fully, from that description we have of it (Rom. 7), how it will darken the mind, extinguish convictions, dethrone reason, interrupt the power and influence of any considerations that may be brought to hamper it, and through all break into a flame. But this is not my present business. Now the first thing in mortification is the weakening of this habit of sin or lust, so that it shall not, with that violence, earnestness, frequency, rise up, conceive, tumultuate, provoke, entice, disquiet, as naturally it is apt to do (Jas. 1:14, 15).

I shall desire to give one caution or rule by the way; and it is this. Though every lust doth, in its own nature, equally, universally incline and impel to sin, yet this must be granted with these two limitations.

The first is, that one lust, or a lust in one man, may receive many accidental improvements, heightenings and strengthenings, which may give it life, power and vigour, exceedingly above what another lust, or the same lust that is of the same kind and nature, hath in another man. When a lust falls in with the natural constitution and temper, with a suitable course of life, with occasions; or when Satan hath got a fit handle to it to manage it, as he hath a thousand ways to do; that lust grows violent and impetuous above others, or more than the same lust in another man. Then the streams of it so darken the mind, that though a man knows the same things as formerly, yet they have no power nor influence on the will, but corrupt affections and passions are set by it at liberty.

But especially, lust gets strength by temptation: when a suitable temptation falls in with a lust, it gives it a new life, vigour, power, violence and rage, which it seemed not before to have, or to be capable of. Instances to this purpose might be multiplied; but it is the design of some part of another treatise to evince this observation.

The second is, that some lusts are far more sensible and discernible in their violent actings than others. Paul puts a difference between uncleanness and all other sins; 'Flee fornication; every sin that a man doth, is without the body, but he that committeth fornication sinneth against his own body' (1 Cor. 6:18). Hence the motions of that sin are more sensible, more discernible than of others. When the love of the world, perhaps, or the like, is no less habitually predominant in a person than that, yet it makes not so great a combustion in the whole man.

And on this account some men may go, in their own thoughts and in the eyes of the world, for mortified men, who yet have in themselves no less predominancy of lust than those who cry out with astonishment upon account of its perplexing tumultuatings – yea, than those who have by the power of it been hurried into scandalous sins; only their lusts are in and about things which raise not such a tumult in the soul, about which they are exercised with a calmer frame of spirit; the very fabric of nature being not so nearly concerned in them as in some other.

I say then that the first thing in mortification is the weakening of this habit, that it shall not impel and tumultuate as formerly, that it shall not entice and draw aside, that it shall not disquiet and perplex: the killing of its life, vigour, promptness and readiness to be stirring. This is called 'crucifying the flesh with the lusts thereof' (Gal. 5:24); that is, taking away its blood and spirits that give it strength and power, the wasting of the body of death day by day (2 Cor. 4:16). As a man nailed to the cross first struggles and strives, and cries out with great strength and might, but as his blood and spirits waste, his strivings are but faint and seldom, his cries low and hoarse, scarce to be heard: so, when a man first sets on a lust or distemper to deal with it, it struggles with great violence to break loose, it cries with earnestness and impatience to be satisfied and relieved; but when, by mortification, the blood and spirits of it are let out, it moves seldom and faintly, cries sparingly, and is scarce heard in the heart: it may have sometimes a dying pang, that makes an appearance of great vigour and strength, but it is quickly over, especially if it be kept from considerable success.

This the apostle describes (Rom. 6) as in the whole chapter, so especially in verse 6. Sin, saith he, is crucified, it is fastened to the cross. To what end? That the body of death may be destroyed; the power of sin weakened, and abolished by little and little; that 'henceforth we should not serve sin', that is, that sin might not incline, impel us with such efficacy as to make us servants to it, as it hath done heretofore. And this is spoken not only with respect to carnal and sensual affections, or desires of worldly things; not only in respect of the lust of the flesh, the lust of the eyes and the pride of life; but also as to the flesh, which is in the mind and will, in that opposition unto God which is in us by nature. Of what nature soever the troubling distemper may be, by what way soever it act itself out, either by impelling to evil, or hindering from that which is good, the rule is the same. And unless this be done effectually, all after contention will not compass the end aimed at. A man may beat down the bitter fruit from an evil tree, until he is weary; whilst the root abides in strength and vigour, the beating down of the present fruit will not hinder it from bringing forth more. This is the folly of some men. They set themselves with all earnestness and diligence against the appearing eruption of lust; but leaving the principle and root untouched, perhaps unsearched out, they make but little or no progress in this work of mortification.

2. *In constant fighting and contending against sin.*
To be able always to be laying load on sin, is no small degree of mortification. When sin is strong and vigorous, the soul is scarce able to make any head against it. It sighs and groans and mourns, and is troubled, as David speaks of himself, but seldom has sin in pursuit. David complains that his sin had 'taken fast hold upon him, that he could not look up' (Ps. 40:12). How little then was he able to fight against it? Now sundry things are required unto, and comprised in, this fighting against sin.

(1) To know that a man hath such an enemy to deal with, to take notice of it, to consider it as an enemy indeed, and one that is to be destroyed by all means possible, is required hereunto. As I said before, the contest is vigorous and hazardous; it is about the things of eternity. When, therefore, men have slight and

transient thoughts of their lusts, it is no great sign that they are mortified, or that they are in a way for their mortification. This is 'every man's knowing the plague of his own heart' (1 Kgs. 8:38), without which no other work can be done. It is to be feared that very many have little knowledge of the main enemy that they carry about them in their bosoms. This makes them ready to justify themselves, and to be impatient of reproof or admonition, not knowing that they are in any danger (2 Chron. 16:10).

(2) To labour to be acquainted with the ways, wiles, methods, advantages and occasions of its success, is the beginning of this warfare. So do men deal with enemies. They inquire out their counsels and designs, ponder their ends, consider how and by what means they have formerly prevailed, that they may get the start of them. In this consists the greatest skill in conduct. Take this away, and all waging of war (wherein is the greatest improvement of human wisdom and industry) would be brutish. So do those deal with lust who mortify it indeed. Not only when it is actually vexing, enticing and seducing; but in their retirements, they consider: This is our enemy, this is his way and progress, these are his advantages, thus hath he prevailed, and thus he will do if not prevented. So David: 'My sin is ever before me' (Ps. 51:3). And indeed, one of the choicest and most eminent parts of practical, spiritual wisdom consists in finding out the subtleties, policies and depths of any indwelling sin. To consider and know wherein its greatest strength

lies; what advantage it is wont to make of occasions, opportunities, temptations; what are its pleas, pretences, reasonings; what its stratagems, colours, excuses; to set the wisdom of the Spirit against the craft of the old man; to trace this serpent in all its turnings and windings; to be able to say at its most secret and (to a common frame of heart) imperceptible actings: 'This is your old way and course, I know what you aim at'; and so to be always in readiness; this is a good part of our warfare.

(3) To load it daily with all the things which shall after be mentioned, that are grievous, killing and destructive to it, is the height of this contest. Such a one never thinks his lust dead because it is quiet; but labours still to give it new wounds, new blows, every day. So the apostle (Col. 3:5).

Now whilst the soul is in this condition, whilst it is thus dealing, it is certainly uppermost; sin is under the sword, and dying.

3. Mortification *consists in success*: frequent success against any lust is another part and evidence of mortification.

By success, I understand not a mere disappointment of sin that it be not brought forth nor accomplished, but a victory over it and pursuit of it to a complete conquest: for instance, when finding sin at any time at work, seducing, forming imaginations to make provision for the flesh to fulfil the lusts thereof, the heart instantly apprehends sin, and brings it to the law of God and love of Christ, condemns it, follows it with execution to the uttermost.

Now I say when a man comes to this state and condition that lust is weakened in the root and principle, that its motions and actions are fewer and weaker than formerly, so that they are not able to hinder his duty nor interrupt his peace; when he can, in a quiet, sedate frame of spirit, find out and fight against sin, and have success against it; then sin is mortified in some considerable measure, and notwithstanding all its opposition, a man may have peace with God all his days.

Unto these heads, then, do I refer the mortification aimed at: that is, of any one perplexing distemper, whereby the general pravity and corruption of our nature attempts to exert and put forth itself.

First, the foundation of it is the weakening of its indwelling disposition, whereby it inclines, entices, impels to evil, rebels, opposes, fights against God; by the implanting, habitual residence and cherishing of a principle of grace, that stands in direct opposition to it, and is destructive of it. So, by the implanting and growth of humility is pride weakened, passion by patience, uncleanness by purity of mind and conscience, love of this world by heavenly-mindedness; which are graces of the Spirit, or the same habitual grace variously acting itself by the Holy Ghost, according to the variety or diversity of the objects about which it is exercised; even as the other are several lusts, or the same natural corruption variously acting itself, according to the various advantages and occasions that it meets withal.

Secondly, the promptness, alacrity, vigour of the Spirit, or new man, in contending with, cheerfully fighting against, the lust spoken of, by all the ways and with all the means that are appointed thereto. Constantly using the succours provided against its motions and actings, is a second thing hereunto required.

Thirdly, success unto several degrees attends these two. Now this, if the distemper hath not an unconquerable advantage from its natural situation, may possibly be to such a universal conquest as that the soul may never more sensibly feel its opposition; but at least that it shall assuredly arise to an allowance of peace to the conscience, according to the tenor of the covenant of grace.

CHAPTER 7

General rules, without which no lust will be mortified.
No mortification unless a man be a believer. Dangers of
attempting mortification of sin by unregenerate persons.
The duty of unconverted persons, as to this business of
mortification, considered. The vanity of the papists'
attempts, and rules for mortification thence discovered.

The ways and means come next to be considered, whereby a soul may proceed to the mortification of any particular lust and sin, of which Satan takes advantage to disquiet and weaken him.

Now there are some general considerations to be premised, concerning some principles and foundations of this work, without which no man in the world, be he ever so much raised by convictions and resolved for the mortification of any sin, can attain thereunto: which was the second thing before proposed.

General rules and principles, without which no sin will ever be mortified, are these:

First: Unless a man be a believer, that is, one that is truly ingrafted into Christ, he can never mortify any one sin. I do not say, unless he knows himself to be so, but unless he indeed be so. Mortification is the work of believers: 'if ye through the Spirit ...' (Rom. 8:13): ye believers, to whom there is no condemnation (v. 1). They alone are exhorted to it: 'Mortify therefore your members that are upon the earth' (Col. 3:5). Who should mortify? You who are risen with Christ (v. 1); whose life is hid with Christ in God (v. 3); who shall appear with him in glory (v. 4). An unregenerate man may do something like it; but the work itself, so as it may be acceptable with God, he can never perform.

You know what a picture of it is drawn in some of the philosophers, Seneca, Tully, Epictetus; what affectionate discourses they have of the contempt of the world and self, of regulating and conquering all exorbitant affections and passions. The lives of most of them manifested that their maxims differed as much from true mortification as the sun painted on a sign-post from the sun in the firmament. They had neither light nor heat. Their own Lucian sufficiently manifests what they all were. There is no death of sin, without the death of Christ.

You know what attempts there are made after it by the papists in their vows, penances and satisfactions; I dare say of them (I mean as many of them as act upon the principles of their church, as they call it), what Paul says of Israel in point of righteousness (Rom. 9:31, 32). They have followed after mortification, but they have not attained to it. Wherefore? Because they 'seek it not by faith, but as it were by the works of the law'. The same is the state and condition of all amongst ourselves, who, in obedience to their convictions and awakened consciences, do attempt a relinquishment of sin; they follow after it, but they do not attain it.

It is true that it is, it will be, required of every person whatever that hears the law or gospel preached, that he mortify sin: it is his duty, but it is not his immediate duty; it is his duty to do it, but to do it in God's way. If you require your servant to pay so much money for you in such a place, but first to go and take it up in another, it is his duty to pay the money appointed, and you will blame him if he do it not: yet it was not his immediate duty; he was first to take it up, according to your direction. So it is in this case; sin is to be mortified, but something is to be done in the first place to enable us thereunto.

I have proved that it is the Spirit alone that can mortify sin. He is promised to do it, and all other means without him are empty and vain. How shall he, then, mortify sin, who hath not the Spirit? A man may easier see without eyes, speak without a tongue, than truly mortify one sin without the Spirit. Now, how is he attained? It is the Spirit of Christ; and, as the apostle says, 'if we have not the Spirit of Christ, we are none of his' (Rom. 8:9); so, if we are Christ's, have an interest in him, we have the Spirit, and so alone have power for mortification. This the apostle discourses of at large (Rom. 8:5-8). 'So then they that are in the flesh cannot please God' (v. 8). This is the inference and conclusion he makes of his foregoing discourse about our natural state and condition, and the enmity we have unto God and his law therein. If we are in the flesh, if we have not the Spirit, we cannot do any thing that should please God.

But what is our deliverance from this condition? 'But ye are not in the flesh, but in the Spirit, if so be that the Spirit of God dwell in you' (v. 9); ye believers, that have the Spirit of Christ, ye are not in the flesh. There is no way of deliverance from the state and condition of being in the flesh but by the Spirit of Christ. And what if this Spirit of Christ be in you? Why then you are mortified, 'the body is dead because of sin' (v. 10), or unto it; mortification is carried on; the new man is quickened to righteousness. This the apostle proves (v. 11) from the union we have with Christ by the Spirit, which will produce operations in us suitable to what it wrought in him. All attempts, then, for mortification of any lust, without an interest in Christ, are vain.

Many men that are galled with sin, and for it (the arrows of Christ for conviction, by the preaching of the word or some affliction, having been made sharp in their hearts), do vigorously set themselves against this or that particular lust, wherewith their consciences have been most disquieted or perplexed. But, poor creatures! they labour in the fire, and their work consumeth.

When the Spirit of Christ comes to this work, he will be 'as a refiner's fire and as fuller's soap', and he will 'purge men as gold and silver' (Mal. 3:3); he will take away their 'dross and tin', their 'filth and blood'

(Isa. 1:25; 4:3). But men must be gold and silver at bottom, or else refining will do them no good. The prophet gives us the sad issue of wicked men's utmost attempts for mortification, by what means soever God affords them: 'The bellows are burned, and the lead is consumed of the fire; the founder melteth in vain; reprobate silver shall men call them, because the Lord hath rejected them' (Jer. 6:29, 30). And what is the reason hereof? They were brass and iron when they were put into the furnace (v. 28). Men may refine brass and iron long enough before they will be good silver.

I say, then, mortification is not the present business of unregenerate men. God calls them not to it as yet. Conversion is their work; the conversion of the whole soul, not the mortification of this or that particular lust. You would laugh at a man that you see setting up a great fabric, and never taking any care for a foundation; especially if you should see him so foolish, as that, having a thousand experiences that what he built one day fell down another, he would yet continue in the same course. So it is with convinced persons: though they plainly see that what ground they get against sin one day they lose another, yet they will go on in the same road still, without inquiring where the destructive flaw in their progress lies.

When the Jews, upon the conviction of their sin, were cut to the heart (Acts 2:37), and cried out, 'What shall we do?' what doth Peter direct them to? Does he bid them go and mortify their pride, wrath, malice, cruelty and the like? No, he knew that was not their present work; but he calls them to conversion, and faith in Christ in general (v. 38). Let their souls be first thoroughly converted, and then, looking on him whom they have pierced, humiliation and mortification will ensue. Thus when John came to preach repentance and conversion, he said, 'The axe is now laid unto the root of the tree' (Matt. 3:10). The Pharisees had been laying heavy burdens, imposing tedious duties and rigid means of mortification, in fastings, washings and the like: all in vain. Says John: The doctrine of conversion is for you; the axe in my hand is laid to the root. And our Saviour tells us what is to be done in this case: 'Do men,' says he, 'gather grapes of thorns?' (Matt. 7:16). But suppose a thorn be well pruned and cut, and have pains taken with him? Yea, but he will never bear figs (vv. 17, 18); it cannot be but every tree will bring forth fruit according to its own kind. What is then to be done? He tells us: 'Make the tree good, and its fruit will be good' (Matt. 12:33). The root must be dealt with, the nature of the tree changed, or no good fruit will be brought forth.

This is that I aim at. Unless a man be regenerate, unless he be a believer, all attempts that he can make for mortification, be they ever so specious and promising; all means he can use, let him follow them with ever so much diligence, earnestness, watchfulness, and contention of mind and spirit; are to no purpose. In vain shall he use many remedies, he shall not be healed. Yea, there are sundry desperate evils attending an endeavour in convinced persons, that are no more but so, to perform this duty.

(1) The mind and soul are taken up about that which is not the man's proper business, and so he is diverted from that which is. God lays hold, by his word and judgments, on some sin in him; galls his conscience, disquiets his heart, deprives him of his rest; now other diversions will not serve his turn, he must apply himself to the work before him. The business in hand being to awake the whole man to a consideration of the state and condition wherein he is, that he might be brought home to God; instead hereof, he sets himself to mortify the sin that galls him; which is a pure issue of self-love, that he may be freed from his trouble, and not at all the work he is called unto; and so he is diverted from it. Thus God tells us of Ephraim, when he 'spread his net upon them', and 'brought them down as the fowls of heaven, and chastised them' (Hos. 7:12), when he caught them, entangled them, convinced them, so that they could not escape: saith he of them, 'They return, but not to the Most High'; they set themselves to a relinquishment of sin, but not in that manner as God called for it, by universal conversion. Thus are men diverted from coming unto God in the most glorious ways that they can fix upon to come to him by. And this is one of the most common deceits whereby men ruin their own souls.

I wish that some whose trade it is to daub with untempered mortar in the things of God, did not teach this deceit, and cause the people to err by their ignorance. What do men do? What, oftentimes, are they directed unto, when their consciences are galled by sin, and disquietment from the Lord hath laid hold upon them? Is not a relinquishment, in practice, of the sin with which in some fruits of it they are perplexed, and to make head against, the sum of what they apply themselves unto? And is not the gospel end of their convictions lost thereby? Here men abide and perish.

(2) This duty, in its proper place, being a good thing in itself, a duty evidencing sincerity, bringing home peace to the conscience; a man, finding himself really engaged in it, his mind and heart set against this or that sin, with purpose and resolution to have no more to do with it, is ready to conclude that his state and condition is good, and so to delude his own soul. For,

(i) When his conscience hath been made sick with sin and he could find no rest, when he should go to the great Physician of souls and get healing in his blood, the man pacifies and quiets his conscience by this engagement against sin, and sits down without going to Christ at all. Ah! how many poor souls are thus deluded to eternity! When 'Ephraim saw his sickness, he sent to king Jareb', which kept him off from God (Hos. 5:13). The whole bundle of the popish religion is made up of designs and contrivances to pacify conscience without Christ: all described by the apostle (Rom. 10:4).

(ii) By this means men satisfy themselves that their state and condition is good, seeing they do that which is a work good in itself, and they do not do it to be seen. They know they would have the work done in sincerity, and so are hardened in a kind of self-righteousness.

(3) When a man hath thus for a season been deluded and hath deceived his own soul, and finds, in a long course of life, that indeed his sin is not mortified, or that if he hath changed one, he hath gotten another; he begins at length to think that all contending is in vain, that he shall never be able to prevail; he is making a dam against water that increaseth on him. Hereupon he gives over, as one despairing of any success; and yields up himself to the power of sin, and that habit of formality that he hath gotten.

And this is the usual issue with persons attempting the mortification of sin, without an interest in Christ first obtained. It deludes them, hardens them, destroys them. And therefore we see that, usually, there are not more vile and desperate sinners in the world than such as having by conviction been put on this course, have found it fruitless, and deserted it without a discovery of Christ. And this is the substance of the religion and godliness of the choicest formalists in the world, and of all those who, in the Roman synagogue, are drawn to mortification as they drive Indians to baptism, or cattle to water. I say then, that mortification is the work of believers, and believers only. To kill sin is the work of living men; where men are dead, as are all unbelievers (even the best of them), sin is alive, and will live. It is the work of faith, the peculiar work of faith; now if there be a work to be done that will be affected by only one instrument, it is the greatest madness for any to attempt the doing of it who hath not that instrument. Now it is faith that purifies the heart (Acts 15:9); or, as Peter speaks, 'we purify our souls in obeying the truth through the Spirit' (1 Pet. 1:22); and without it, it will not be done.

What hath been spoken, I suppose, is sufficient to make good my first general rule: Be sure to get an interest in Christ, if you intend to mortify any sin; without it, it will never be done.

Objection. You will say: What then would you have unregenerate men, that are convinced of the evil of sin, to do? Shall they cease striving against sin, live dissolutely, give their lusts their swing, and be as bad as the worst of men? This were a way to set the whole world into confusion, to bring all things into darkness, to set open the flood-gates of lusts, and lay the reins upon the necks of men to rush into all sin with delight and greediness, like the horse into the battle.

Answer 1. God forbid! It is to be looked on as a great issue of the wisdom, goodness and love of God that, by manifold ways and means, he is pleased to restrain the sons of men from running forth into that compass of excess and riot, which the depravity of their nature would carry them out unto with violence. By what way soever this is done, it is an issue of the care, kindness and goodness of God, without which the whole earth would be a hell of sin and confusion.

Answer 2. There is a peculiar convincing power in the Word, which God is oftentimes pleased to put forth, to the wounding, amazing, and, in some sort, humbling of sinners, though they are never converted. And the Word is to be preached, yet not with this end, though it hath this end. Let, then, the Word be preached, and the sins of men rebuked; lust will be restrained, and some oppositions will be made against sin, though that be not the effect aimed at.

Answer 3. Though this be the work of the Word and Spirit, and it be good in itself, yet it is not profitable nor available as to the main end in them in whom it is wrought; they are still in the gall of bitterness and under the power of darkness.

Answer 4. Let me know it is their duty, but in its proper place. I take not men from mortification, but put them upon conversion. He that shall call a man from mending a hole in the wall of his house, to quench a fire that is consuming the whole building, is not his enemy. Poor soul! it is not thy sore finger, but thy hectic fever, that thou art to apply thyself to the consideration of. Thou settest thyself against a particular sin, and dost not consider that thou art nothing but sin.

Let me add this to them who are preachers of the Word, or intend through the good hand of God that employment. It is their duty to plead with men about their sins, and to lay load on particular sins; but always to remember that it be done with that which is the proper end of law and gospel; that is, that they make use of the sin they speak against, to the discovery of the state and condition wherein the sinner is. Otherwise, they may haply work men to formality and hypocrisy, but little of the true end of preaching the gospel will be brought about. It will not avail to beat a man off from his drunkenness into a sober formality: a skilful master of the assemblies lays his axe at the root, drives still at the heart. To inveigh against particular sins of ignorant, unregenerate persons, such as the land is full of, is a good work: but yet, though it may be done with great efficacy, vigour and success, if all the effect of it be this, that they are set upon the most sedulous endeavours to mortify their sins preached down, all that is done is but like the beating of an enemy in an open field, and driving him into an impregnable castle not to be prevailed against. Get you a sinner at any time at the advantage on account of any one sin whatever; have you any thing to take hold of him by; bring it to his state and condition, drive it up to the head, and there deal with him. To break men off from particular sins, and not to break their hearts, is to deprive ourselves of advantages of dealing with them.

And herein is the Roman mortification grievously faulty; they drive all sorts of persons to it, without the least consideration whether they have a principle for it or no. Yea, they are so far from calling on men to believe, in order that they may be able to mortify their lusts, that they call men to mortification instead of believing. The truth is, they neither know what it is to believe, nor what mortification itself intends. Faith with them is but a general assent to the doctrine taught in their church; and mortification is the betaking of a man by a vow to some certain course of life, wherein he denies himself something of the use of the things of this world, not without a considerable compensation. Such men know neither the Scriptures nor the power of God. Their boasting of their mortification is but their glorying in their shame.

Some casuists among ourselves, who overlooking the necessity of regeneration, do avowedly give this for a direction to all sorts of persons who complain of any sin or lust, that they should vow against it, at least for a season, a month or so, seem to have a scantling of light in the mystery of the gospel, much like that of Nicodemus when he came first to Christ. They bid men vow to abstain from their sin for a season. This commonly makes their lust more impetuous. Perhaps with great perplexity they keep their word: perhaps not, which increases their guilt and torment. Is their sin at all mortified hereby? Do they find a conquest over it? Is their condition changed, though they attain a relinquishment of it? Are they not still in the gall of bitterness? Is not this to put men to make brick, if not without straw yet, which is worse, without strength? What promise hath any unregenerate man to countenance him in this work? What assistance for the performance of it? Can sin be killed without an interest in the death of Christ, or mortified without the Spirit? If such directions should prevail to change men's lives, as seldom they do, yet they never reach to the change of their hearts or conditions. They make men self-justifiers or hypocrites, not Christians.

It grieves me oftentimes to see poor souls, that have a zeal for God and a desire of eternal welfare, kept by such directors and directions, under a hard, burdensome, outside worship and service of God, with many specious endeavours for mortification, in an utter ignorance of the righteousness of Christ, and un-acquaintedness with his Spirit, all their days. Persons and things of this kind, I know too many. If ever God shine into their hearts to give them the knowledge of his glory in the face of his Son Jesus Christ, they will see the folly of their present way.

CHAPTER 8

*The second general rule proposed. Without universal
sincerity for the mortifying of every lust, no lust will be
mortified. Partial mortification always from a corrupt
principle. Perplexity of temptation from a lust, oftentimes
a chastening for other negligences.*

The *second* principle which I shall propose to this
purpose is this: Without sincerity and diligence
in the universality of obedience, there is no
mortification of any one perplexing lust to be obtained.
The former was to the person, this to the thing itself.
I shall a little explain this position.

A man finds any lust to bring him into the condition
formerly described; it is powerful, strong, tumultuating, leads captive, vexes, disquiets, takes away
peace. He is not able to bear it; wherefore he sets
himself against it, prays against it, groans under it, sighs
to be delivered. But in the mean time, perhaps in other
duties, in constant communion with God, in reading,
prayer, and meditation, in other ways that are not of

the same kind with the lust wherewith he is troubled, he is loose and negligent. Let not that man think that ever he shall arrive to the mortification of the lust he is perplexed with.

This is a condition that not seldom befalls men in their pilgrimage. The Israelites, under a sense of their sin, drew nigh to God with much diligence and earnestness, with fasting and prayer (Isa. 58). Many expressions are used of their earnestness in the work: 'They seek me daily, and delight to know my ways; they ask of me the ordinances of justice; they delight in approaching unto God' (v. 2). But God rejects all; their fast is a remedy that will not heal them: and the reason given of it in verses 5-7 is because they were exclusive in this duty; they attended diligently to it, but in others were negligent and careless. He that hath (it is the Scripture expression) a running sore upon him, arising from an ill habit of body contracted by intemperance and ill diet, let him apply himself with what diligence and skill he can to the cure of his sore, if he leave the general habit of his body under distempers, his labour and travail will be in vain. So will his attempts be that shall endeavour to stop a bloody issue of sin and filth in his soul, and is not equally careful of his universal spiritual temperament and constitution. For,

(1) This kind of endeavour for mortification proceeds from a corrupt principle, ground and foundation: so that it will never proceed to a good issue. The true and acceptable principles of mortification shall be

afterward insisted on. Hatred of sin as sin, not only as galling or disquieting; a sense of the love of Christ in the cross; lie at the bottom of all true spiritual mortification. Now it is certain that that which I speak of proceeds from self-love. Thou settest thyself with all diligence and earnestness to mortify such a lust or sin: what is the reason of it? It disquiets thee; it hath taken away thy peace; it fills thy heart with sorrow and trouble and fear; thou hast no rest because of it. Yea, but, friend, thou hast neglected prayer or reading; thou hast been vain and loose in thy conversation, in other things that have not been of the same nature with that lust wherewith thou art perplexed; these are no less sins and evils than those under which thou groanest; Jesus Christ bled for them also: why dost thou not set thyself against them also? If thou hatest sin as sin, every evil way, thou wouldest be no less watchful against every thing that grieves and disquiets the Spirit of God, than against that which grieves and disquiets thine own soul. It is evident that thou contendest against sin merely because of thine own trouble by it. Would thy conscience be quiet under it, thou wouldest let it alone. Did it not disquiet thee, it should not be disquieted by thee.

Now, canst thou think that God will go along with such hypocritical endeavours, that ever his Spirit will bear witness to the treachery and falsehood of thy spirit? Dost thou think he will ease thee of that which perplexeth thee, that thou mayest be at liberty to do that which no less grieves him? No, says God, here is one of whom, if he could be rid of this lust, I should

never hear more; let him wrestle with this, or he is
lost. Let not any man think to do his own work, that
will not do God's. God's work consists in universal
obedience: to be freed of the present perplexity is their
own only. Hence is that of the apostle: 'Cleanse
yourselves from all pollution of flesh and spirit,
perfecting holiness in the fear of the Lord' (2 Cor. 7:1).
If we will do any thing, we must do all things. So then,
it is not only an intense opposition to this or that
peculiar lust, but a universal humble frame and temper
of heart, with watchfulness over every evil, and for
the performance of every duty, that is accepted.

(2) How knowest thou, but that God hath suffered the
lust wherewith thou hast been perplexed to get
strength in thee and power over thee, to chasten thee
for thy other negligences and common lukewarmness
in walking before him: at least, to awaken thee to the
consideration of thy ways that thou mayest make a
thorough work and change in thy course of walking
with him? The rage and predominancy of a particular
lust is commonly the fruit and issue of a careless,
negligent course in general; and that upon a double
account:

(i) As its natural effect, if I may so say. Lust, as I
showed in general, lies in the heart of every one, even
the best, whilst he lives: and think not that the Scripture
speaks in vain, that it is subtle, cunning, crafty; that it
seduces, entices, fights, rebels. Whilst a man keeps a
diligent watch over his heart, its root and fountain;
whilst, above all keepings, he keeps his heart whence

are the issues of life and death; lust withers and dies in it. But if, through negligence, it makes an eruption any particular way, gets a passage to the thoughts by the affections and, from them and by them, perhaps breaks out into open sin in the conversation; the strength of it bears that way it hath found out, and that way mainly it urgeth; until, having got a passage, it then vexes and disquiets, and is not easily to be restrained. Thus, perhaps, a man may be put to wrestle all his days in sorrow with that which by a strict, universal watch might easily have been prevented.

(ii) As I said, God oftentimes suffers it to chasten our other negligences. For, as with wicked men, he gives them up to one sin as the judgment of another (Rom. 1:26), to a greater for the punishment of a less, or one that will hold them more firmly and securely for that from which they might have possibly obtained a deliverance; so even with his own, he may, he doth, leave them sometimes to some vexatious distempers, either to prevent or cure some other evil. So was the messenger of Satan let loose on Paul, that he might not be lifted up through the abundance of spiritual revelations (2 Cor. 12:7). Was it not a correction to Peter's vain confidence, that he was left to deny his Master?

Now if this be the state and condition of lust in its prevalency, that God oftentimes suffers it thus to prevail, at least to admonish us and to humble us, perhaps to chasten and correct us, for our general loose and careless walking; is it possible that the effect should be removed and the cause continued, that the particular lust should be mortified, and the general course be unreformed? He, then, that would really, thoroughly and acceptably mortify any disquieting lust, let him take care to be equally diligent in all parts of obedience; and know that every lust, every omission of duty, is burdensome to God, though but one is so to him (Isa. 43:24). Whilst there abides a treachery in the heart to give indulgence to any negligence, in not pressing universally to all perfection in obedience; the soul is weak, as not giving faith its whole work, and selfish, as considering more the trouble of sin than the filth and guilt of it; and lives under a constant provocation of God, so that it may not expect any comfortable issue in any spiritual duty that it doth undertake, much less in this under consideration, which requires another principle and frame of spirit for its accomplishment.

CHAPTER 9

Particular directions in relation to the foregoing case proposed. First, Consider the dangerous symptoms of any lust: 1. Inveterateness. 2. Peace obtained under it; the several ways whereby that is done. 3. Frequency of success in its seductions. 4. The soul's fighting against it with arguments taken only from the event. 5. Its being attended with judiciary hardness. 6. Its withstanding particular dealings from God. The state of persons in whom these things are found.

Third: The foregoing general rules being supposed, particular directions to the soul for its guidance under the sense of a disquieting lust or distemper, come next to be proposed; which is the main thing I aim at. Now of these some are previous and preparatory, and in some of them the work itself is contained.

1. Of the first sort are these ensuing.

Direction 1: Consider what dangerous symptoms thy lust hath attending or accompanying it: whether it hath any deadly mark on it or no. If it hath, extraordinary remedies are to be used; an ordinary course of mortification will not do it.

You will say: What are these dangerous marks and symptoms, the desperate attendances of an indwelling lust, that you intend? Some of them I shall name.

(1) *Inveterateness.* If it hath lain long corrupting in thy heart, if thou hast suffered it to abide in power and prevalency for some long season, without attempting vigorously the killing of it, and the healing of the wounds thou hast received by it, thy distemper is dangerous. Hast thou, for some long season, permitted worldliness, ambition, greediness of study, to eat up other duties, the duties wherein thou oughtest to hold constant communion with God? Or uncleanness to defile thy heart, with vain and foolish, and wicked imaginations, for many days? Thy lust hath a dangerous symptom. So was the case with David: 'My wounds stink and are corrupt, because of my foolishness' (Ps. 38:5). When a lust hath lain long in the heart, corrupting, festering, cankering, it brings the soul to a woeful condition. In such a case an ordinary course of humiliation will not do the work. For, whatever it will be, it will, by the means foregoing, insinuate itself more or less into all the faculties of the soul, and habituate the affections to its company and society; it grows familiar to the mind and conscience, that they do not startle at it as a strange thing, but are bold with it as that which they are wonted unto; yea, it will get such advantage by this means, as oftentimes to exert

and put forth itself without having any notice taken of it at all, as it seems to have been with Joseph in his swearing by the life of Pharaoh. Unless some extraordinary course be taken, such a person hath no ground in the world to expect that his latter end shall be peace.

For, first, how will he be able to distinguish between the long abode of an unmortified lust and the dominion of sin which cannot befall a regenerate person? Secondly, how can he promise himself that it shall ever be otherwise with him, or that his lusts will cease tumultuating and seducing, when he sees that it is fixed and abiding, and hath been so for many days, and hath gone through a variety of conditions with him? It may be it hath tried mercies and afflictions, and those possibly so remarkable that the soul could not avoid taking special notice of them: it may be it hath weathered out many a storm, and passed under much variety of gifts in the administration of the word. And will it prove an easy thing to dislodge an inmate pleading a title by prescription? Old neglected wounds are often mortal, always dangerous. Indwelling distemper grows restive and stubborn, by continuance in ease and quiet. Lust is such an inmate as, if it can plead time and some prescription, will not easily be ejected. As it never dies of itself, so, if it be not daily killed, it will always gather strength.

(2) Secret pleas of the heart for countenancing itself and keeping up its peace, notwithstanding the abiding of a lust, without a vigorous gospel attempt for its mortification are another dangerous symptom of a

deadly distemper in the heart. Now there are several ways whereby this may be done. I shall name some of them. As,

[i] When upon thoughts, perplexing thoughts about sin, instead of applying himself to the destruction of it, a man searches his heart to see what evidences he can find of a good condition notwithstanding that sin and lust, so that it may go well with him.

For a man to gather up his experiences of God, to call them to mind, to collect them, to consider, try, improve them, is an excellent thing, a duty practised by all the saints, commended in the Old Testament and the New. This was David's work, when he 'communed with his own heart', and called to remembrance the former loving-kindness of the Lord (Ps. 77:6-9). This is the duty that Paul sets us to practise (2 Cor. 13:5). And as it is in itself excellent, so it hath beauty added to it by a proper season. A time of trial, or temptation, or disquietment of the heart about sin, is a picture of silver to set off this golden apple, as Solomon speaks. But now, to do it for this end, to satisfy conscience which cries and calls for another purpose, is a desperate device of a heart in love with sin. When a man's conscience shall deal with him, when God shall rebuke him for the sinful distemper of his heart; if he, instead of applying himself to get that sin pardoned in the blood of Christ and mortified by his Spirit, shall relieve himself by any such other evidences as he hath or thinks himself to have, and so disentangle himself from under the yoke that God was putting on his neck; his condition is very dangerous, his wound hardly curable. Thus the Jews, under the gallings of their own consciences, and the convincing preaching of our Saviour, supported themselves with this, that they were Abraham's children, and on that account accepted with God; and so countenanced themselves in all abominable wickedness to their utter ruin.

This is, in some degree, a 'blessing of a man's self', and saying, upon one account or other, that 'he shall have peace although he adds drunkenness to thirst'. Love of sin, undervaluation of peace and of all tastes of love from God, are inwrapped in such a frame. Such a one plainly shows that if he can but keep up hope of escaping the wrath to come, he can be well content to be unfruitful in the world, at any distance from God that is not final separation. What is to be expected from such a heart?

[ii] By applying grace and mercy to an unmortified sin, or one not sincerely endeavoured to be mortified, is this deceit carried on. This is a sign of a heart greatly entangled with the love of sin. When, like Naaman about his worshipping in the house of Rimmon (2 Kgs. 5:18), a man hath secret thoughts in his heart, 'In all other things I will walk with God, but, in this thing, God be merciful unto me!' his condition is sad. It is true, indeed, a resolution to this purpose to indulge a man's self in any sin on the account of mercy, seems to be (and doubtless, if for any course, is) altogether inconsistent with Christian sincerity, is a badge of a hypocrite and is the turning of the grace of God into wantonness (Jude 4); yet I doubt not but, through the craft of Satan and their own remaining unbelief, the

children of God may themselves sometimes be ensnared with this deceit of sin; or else Paul would never have so cautioned them against it as he doth (Rom. 6:1, 2). Yea, indeed, there is nothing more natural than for fleshly reasonings to grow high and strong on this account. The flesh would fain be indulged upon the account of grace: and every word that is spoken of mercy, it stands ready to catch at, and to pervert to its own corrupt aims and purposes. To apply mercy, then, to a sin not vigorously mortified is to fulfil the end of the flesh upon the gospel.

These and many other ways and wiles, a deceitful heart will sometimes make use of, to countenance itself in its abominations. Now, when a man with his sin is in this condition, and there is a secret liking of the sin prevalent in his heart, so that, though his will be not wholly set upon it, yet he hath an imperfect willingness towards it, would practise it were it not for such and such considerations, and hereupon relieves himself other ways than by the mortification and pardon of it in the blood of Christ; that man's wounds stink and are corrupt, and he will, without speedy deliverance, be at the door of death.

(3) Frequency of success in sin's seduction, in obtaining the prevailing consent of the will unto it, is another dangerous symptom. This is that I mean: when the sin spoken of gets the consent of the will with some delight, though it be not actually outwardly perpetrated, yet it hath success. A man may not be able, upon outward considerations, to go along with

sin, to that which James, in chapter 1:14, 15, calls the finishing of it, as to the outward acts, when yet the will to sin may be actually obtained: then hath it, I say, success. Now if any lust be able thus far to prevail in the soul of any man, as his condition may possibly be very bad, and himself be unregenerate, so it cannot possibly be very good, but dangerous. And it is all one as to the matter, whether this be done by the choice of the will or by inadvertency, for that inadvertency itself is in a manner chosen. When we are inadvert and negligent where we are bound to watchfulness and carefulness, that inadvertency does not take off from the voluntariness of what we do thereupon; for although men do not choose and resolve to be negligent and inadvertent, yet if they choose the things that will make them so, they choose inadvertency itself, as a thing may be chosen in its cause.

And let not men think that the evil of their hearts is in any measure extenuated because they seem for the most part to be surprised into that consent which they seem to give unto it; for it is negligence of their duty in watching over their hearts that betrays them into that surprisal.

(4) When a man fighteth against his sin only with arguments from the issue or the punishment due unto it, it is a sign that sin hath taken great possession of the will, and that in the heart there is a superfluity of naughtiness. Such a man as opposes nothing to the seduction of sin and lust in his heart, but fear of shame among men or hell from God, is sufficiently resolved

to do the sin, if there were no punishment attending it; which what it differs from living in the practice of sin, I know not. Those who are Christ's, and are actuated in their obedience upon gospel principles, have the death of Christ, the love of God, the detestable nature of sin, the preciousness of communion with God, a deep-grounded abhorrency of sin as sin, to oppose to any seduction of sin, to all the workings, strivings, fightings of lust in their hearts. So did Joseph (Gen. 39:9): 'How shall I do this great evil,' saith he, 'and sin against the Lord', my good and gracious God? And Paul, 'The love of Christ constrains us' (2 Cor. 5:14); and, 'Having received these promises, let us cleanse ourselves from all pollutions of flesh and spirit' (2 Cor. 7:1). But now, if a man be so under the power of his lust that he hath nothing but law to oppose it with; if he cannot fight against it with gospel weapons, but deals with it altogether with hell and judgment, which are the proper arms of the law; it is most evident that sin hath possessed itself of his will and affections to a very great prevalency and conquest.

Such a person hath, as to the particular spoken of, cast off the conduct of renewing grace, and is kept from ruin only by restraining grace; and so far is he fallen from grace, and returned under the power of the law; and can it be thought that this is not a great provocation to Christ, that men should cast off his easy, gentle yoke and rule, and cast themselves under the iron yoke of the law, merely out of indulgence unto their lusts?

Try thyself by this also. When thou art by sin driven to make a stand, so that thou must either serve it and rush at the command of it into folly, like the horse into the battle, or make head against it to suppress it, what dost thou say to thy soul? Is this all? Hell will be the end of this course, vengeance will meet with me and find me out! It is time for thee to look about thee; evil lies at the door. Paul's main argument to evince that sin shall not have dominion over believers is that they are not under the law, but under grace (Rom. 6:14). If thy contendings against sin be all on legal accounts, from legal principles and motives, what assurance canst thou attain to that sin shall not have dominion over thee, which will be thy ruin?

Yea, know, that this reserve will not long hold out; if thy lust hath driven thee from stronger gospel forts, it will speedily prevail against this also. Do not suppose that such considerations will deliver thee, when thou hast voluntarily given up to thine enemy those helps and means of preservation which have a thousand times their strength. Rest assuredly in this, that unless thou recover thyself with speed from this condition, the thing that thou fearest will come upon thee. What gospel principles do not, legal motives cannot do.

(5) When it is probable that there is, or may be, somewhat of judiciary hardness, or at least chastening punishment, in thy lust as disquieting; this is another dangerous symptom. That God doth sometimes leave even those of his own under the perplexing power of some lust or sin at least, to correct them for former

sins, negligence and folly, I no way doubt. Hence was that complaint of the church, 'Why hast thou hardened us from the fear of thy name?' (Isa. 63:17). That this is his way of dealing with unregenerate men, no man questions. But how shall a man know whether there be any thing of God's chastening hand in his being left to the disquietment of his distemper?

Answer. Examine thy heart and ways. What was the state and condition of thy soul before thou fellest into the entanglements of that sin of which now thou so complainest? Hadst thou been negligent in duties? Hadst thou lived inordinately to thyself? Is there the guilt of any great sin lying upon thee unrepented of? A new sin may be permitted, as well as a new affliction sent, to bring an old sin to remembrance.

Hast thou received any eminent mercy, protection, deliverance, which thou didst not improve in a due manner, nor were thankful for? Or hast thou been exercised with any affliction, without labouring for the appointed end of it? Or hast thou been wanting to the opportunities of glorifying God in thy generation, which in his good providence he had graciously afforded unto thee? Or hast thou conformed thyself unto the world and the men of it, through the abounding of temptations in the days wherein thou livest?

If thou findest this to have been thy state, awake, call upon God; thou art fast asleep in a storm of anger round about thee.

(6) When thy lust hath already withstood particular dealings from God against it. This condition is described: 'For the iniquity of his covetousness I was wroth, and smote him: I hid me, and was wroth, and he went on frowardly in the way of his heart' (Isa. 57:17). God hath dealt with them about their prevailing lust, and that several ways, by affliction and desertion; but they held out against all. This is a sad condition, in which nothing can relieve a man but mere sovereign grace, as God expresses it in the next verse; which no man ought to promise himself, or bear himself upon. God oftentimes, in his providential dispensations, meets with a man and speaks particularly to the evil of his heart, as he did to Joseph's brethren concerning their selling him into Egypt. This makes the man reflect on his sin and judge himself in particular for it. God makes it to be the voice of the danger, affliction, trouble, sickness, that he is in or under. Sometimes, in reading of the Word, God makes a man stay on something that cuts him to the heart, and shakes him as to his present condition. More frequently doth he meet with men, in the hearing of the Word preached, his great ordinance for conviction, conversion and edification. God often hews men by the sword of his Word in that ordinance; strikes directly on their bosom-beloved lust; startles the sinner; makes him engage to the mortification and relinquishment of the evil of his heart.

Now if his lust have taken such hold on him as to enforce him to break these bonds of the Lord, and to cast these cords from him; if it overcomes these convictions, and gets again into its old posture; if it can cure the wounds it so receives; that soul is in a sad condition. Unspeakable are the evils which attend such a frame of heart; every particular warning to a man in such a state is an inestimable mercy; how then doth he despise God in them who holds out against them! And what infinite patience is this in God that he doth not cast off such a one, and swear in his wrath that he shall never enter into his rest!

These and many other evidences are there of a lust that is dangerous, if not mortal. As our Saviour said of the evil spirit, 'This kind goeth not out but by fasting and prayer', so say I of lusts of this kind; an ordinary course of mortification will not do it; extraordinary ways must be fixed on.

This is the first particular direction: Consider whether the lust or sin you are contending with, hath any of these dangerous symptoms attending upon it.

Before I proceed, I must give one caution by the way, lest any be deceived by what hath been spoken. Whereas, I say, the things and evils above-mentioned may befall true believers, let not any that finds the same things in himself, thence conclude that he is a true believer. These are the evils that believers may fall into and be ensnared with, not the things that constitute a believer. A man may as well conclude that he is a believer because he is an adulterer, seeing David, that was so, fell into adultery, as conclude it from the signs foregoing, which are the evils of sin and Satan in the hearts of believers.

The seventh of the Romans contains the description of a regenerate man. He that shall consider what is spoken of his dark side, of his unregenerate part, of the indwelling power and violence of sin remaining in him; and because he finds the like in himself, conclude that he is a regenerate man, will be deceived in his reckoning. It is all one as if you should argue: A wise man may be sick and wounded, yea, do some things foolishly; therefore every one who is sick and wounded, and does things foolishly, is a wise man. Or, as if a silly deformed creature, hearing one say of a beautiful person, that he had a mark or a scar that much disfigured him, should conclude that because he hath himself scars and moles and warts, that he also is beautiful. If you will have evidences of your being believers, it must be from those things that constitute men believers. He that hath these things in himself may safely conclude, 'If I am a believer, I am a most miserable one.' But that any man is so, he must look for other evidences, if he will have peace.

CHAPTER 10

The second particular direction. Get a clear sense of, 1. The guilt of the sin perplexing. Considerations for help therein proposed. 2. Of the danger; manifold. (1) Of hardening. (2) Of temporal correction. (3) Of loss of peace and strength. (4) Of eternal destruction. Rules for the management of this consideration. 3. The evil of it. (1) In grieving the Spirit. (2) In wounding the new creature.

*D*irection 2: Get a clear and abiding sense upon thy mind and conscience, first, of the guilt, secondly, of the danger, thirdly, of the evil, of that sin wherewith thou art perplexed.

1. *Of the guilt of it.*
It is one of the deceits of a prevailing lust, to extenuate its own guilt. Is it not a little one? When I go and bow myself in the house of Rimmon, God be merciful to me in this thing. Though this be bad, yet it is not so bad as such and such an evil; others of the people of

God have had such a frame; yea, what dreadful actual
sins have some of them fallen into! Innumerable ways
there are whereby sin diverts the mind from a right
and due apprehension of its guilt. Its noisome
exhalations darken the mind, so that it cannot make a
right judgment of things: perplexing reasonings,
extenuating promises, tumultuating desires, treach-
erous purposes of relinquishment, hopes of mercy, all
have a share in disturbing the mind in its consideration
of the guilt of a prevailing lust. The prophet tells us,
that lust will do this wholly, when it comes to the
height: 'Whoredom, and wine, and new wine, take
away the heart' (Hos. 4:11); the heart meaning the
understanding, as it is often used in the Scripture.

And as they accomplish this work to the height in
unregenerate persons, so in part in regenerate also.
Solomon tells you of him who was enticed by the lewd
woman, that he was among the simple ones, he was a
'young man void of understanding' (Prov. 7:7). And
wherein did his folly appear? Why, says he, in the 23rd
verse, 'he knew not that it was for his life'; he
considered not the guilt of the evil that he was involved
in. And the Lord, rendering a reason why his dealings
with Ephraim took no better effect, gives this account:
'Ephraim is like a silly dove, without heart' (Hos. 7:11);
he had no understanding of his own miserable
condition. Would it have been possible that David
should have lain so long in the guilt of that abominable
sin, but that he had innumerable corrupt reasonings,
hindering him from taking a clear view of its ugliness
and guilt, in the glass of the law? This made the prophet

that was sent for his awakening, shut up all subterfuges and pretences, in his dealings with him, by his parable; that so he might fall fully under a sense of the guilt of it.

This is the proper issue of lust in the heart; it darkens the mind so that it shall not judge aright of its guilt; and many other ways it hath for its own extenuation, that I shall not now insist on. Let this then be the first care of him that would mortify sin, to fix a right judgment of its guilt in his mind. To which end take these considerations to thy assistance.

(1) Though the power of sin be weakened by inherent grace in them that have it, so that sin shall not have dominion over them as it hath over others, yet the guilt of sin that yet abides and remains is aggravated and heightened by it. 'What shall we say then? Shall we continue in sin that grace may abound? God forbid. How shall we that are dead to sin, live any longer therein?' (Rom. 6:1, 2). 'How shall we that are dead'; the emphasis is on the word *we*. How shall we do it, who, as he afterwards describes it, have received grace from Christ to the contrary? We, doubtless, are more evil than any, if we do it. I shall not insist on the special aggravations of the sins of such persons; how they sin against more love, mercy, grace, assistance, relief, means and deliverances than others. But let this consideration abide in thy mind. There is inconceivably more evil and guilt in the evil of thy heart that doth remain, than there would be in so much sin if thou hadst no grace at all. Observe,

(2) That as God sees abundance of beauty and excellency in the desires of the hearts of his servants, more than in any of the most glorious works of other men, yea, more than in most of their own outward performances, which have a greater mixture of sin than the desires and pantings of grace in the heart have; so God sees a great deal of evil in the working of lust in their hearts, yea, and more than in the open notorious acts of wicked men, or in many outward sins whereinto the saints may fall; seeing there is more opposition made against them, and more humiliation generally follows them. Thus Christ, dealing with his decaying children (Rev. 3:15), goes to the root with them; lays aside their profession; 'I know thee', thou art quite another thing than thou professeth, and this makes thee abominable.

So then, let these things, and the like considerations, lead thee to a clear sense of the guilt of thy indwelling lust, that there may be no room in thy heart for extenuating or excusing thoughts, whereby sin insensibly will get strength and prevail.

2. *Consider the danger of it*, which is manifold:
(1) Of being hardened by its deceitfulness. This the apostle sorely charges on the Hebrews 3:12, 13: 'Take heed, brethren, lest there be in any of you an evil heart of unbelief, in departing from the living God; but exhort one another daily, while it is called today, lest any of you be hardened through the deceitfulness of sin'. Take heed, saith he; use all means, consider your temptations, watch diligently; there is a treachery, a

deceit in sin, that tends to the hardening of your hearts from the fear of God.

The hardening here mentioned is to the utmost, utter obduration: sin tends to it, and every distemper and lust will make at least some progress towards it. Thou that wast tender, and didst use to melt under the Word and under afflictions, wilt grow, as some have profanely spoken, sermon-proof and sickness-proof. Thou that didst tremble at the presence of God, at thoughts of death, and appearance before him, when thou hadst more assurance of his love than now thou hast, shalt have a stoutness upon thy spirit not to be moved by these things. Thy soul and thy sin shall be spoken of and spoken to, and thou shalt not be at all concerned; but shalt be able to pass over duties, praying, hearing, reading, and thy heart not in the least effected. Sin will grow a light thing to thee; thou wilt pass by it as a thing of nought: this it will grow to, and what will be the end of such a condition? Can a sadder thing befall thee? Is it not enough to make any heart to tremble, to think of being brought into that state wherein slight thoughts of sin, slight thoughts of grace, of mercy, of the blood of Christ, of the law, heaven and hell, should come all in at the same season? Take heed; this is that thy lusting is working towards; even to the hardening of the heart, searing of the conscience, blinding of the mind, stupifying of the affections and deceiving of the whole soul.

(2) The danger of some great temporal correction, which the Scripture calls vengeance, judgment and

punishment (Ps. 89:30-33). Though God shall not utterly cast thee off for this abomination that lies in thy heart, yet he will visit with the rod: though he pardon and forgive, he will take vengeance of thy inventions. O remember David and all his troubles! Look on him flying into the wilderness, and consider the hand of God upon him. Is it nothing to thee, that God should kill thy child in anger, ruin thy estate in anger, break thy bones in anger, in anger suffer thee to be a scandal and reproach, in anger kill thee, destroy thee, make thee lie down in darkness? Is it nothing that he should punish, ruin and undo others for thy sake? Let me not be mistaken; I do not mean that God doth send all these things always on his people in anger; God forbid. But this I say, that when he doth so deal with thee, and thy conscience bears witness with him what thy provocations have been, thou wilt find his dealings full of bitterness to thy soul. If thou fearest not these things, I fear thou art under hardness.

(3) The danger of loss of peace and strength, all a man's days. To have peace with God, to have strength to walk before God, is the sum of the great promises of the covenant of grace. In these things is the life of our souls. Without them in some comfortable measure, to live is to die. What good will our lives do us, if we see not the face of God sometimes in peace? if we have not some strength to walk with him? Now, of both these will an unmortified lust certainly deprive the souls of men. This case is so evident in David, as that nothing can be more clear. How often doth he complain that

his bones were broken, his soul disquieted, his wounds grievous, on this account! Take other instances: 'For the iniquity of his covetousness I was wroth, and hid myself' (Isa. 57:18). What peace, I pray, is there to a soul while God hides himself? or strength whilst he smites? 'I will go and return to my place, until they acknowledge their offence, and seek my face' (Hos. 5:15). I will leave them, hide my face, and what will become of their peace and strength? If ever, then, thou hast enjoyed peace with God; if ever his terrors have made thee afraid; if ever thou hast had strength to walk with him, or ever hast mourned in thy prayer, and been troubled because of thy weakness; think of this danger that hangs over thy head.

It is perhaps but a little while, and thou shalt see the face of God in peace no more: perhaps by tomorrow thou shalt not be able to pray, read, hear or perform any duties with the least cheerfulness, life or vigour: and possibly thou mayest never see a quiet hour whilst thou livest; thou mayest carry about thee broken bones full of pain and terror all the days of thy life. Yea, perhaps God will shoot his arrows at thee, and fill thee with anguish and disquietness, with fears and perplexities; make thee a terror and an astonishment to thyself and others; show thee hell and wrath every moment; frighten and scare thee with sad apprehensions of his hatred; so that thy sore shall run in the night season, and thy soul shall refuse comfort; so that thou shalt wish death rather than life, yea, thy soul may choose strangling. Consider this a little, that though God should not utterly destroy thee, yet he might cast thee into this condition, wherein thou shalt have quick and living apprehensions of thy destruction. Accustom thy heart to thoughts hereof; let it be known what it is like to be the issue of its state; leave not this consideration until thou hast made thy soul to tremble within thee.

(4) There is the danger of eternal destruction. For the due management of this consideration, observe, first of all, that there is such a connection between a continuance in sin and eternal destruction, that though God does resolve to deliver some from a continuance in sin that they may not be destroyed, yet he will deliver none from destruction that continue in sin. So that, whilst any one lies under an abiding power of sin, the threats of destruction and everlasting separation from God are to be held out to him. So Hebrews 3:12, to which add Hebrews 10:38. This is the rule of God's proceeding: if any man depart from him, draw back through unbelief, God's soul hath no pleasure in him; that is, his indignation shall pursue him to destruction. So evidently Galatians 6:8.

But again, he who is so entangled, as above described, under the power of any corruption, can have, at that present, no clear, prevailing evidence of his interest in the covenant by the efficacy whereof he may be delivered from fear of destruction. So that, destruction from the Lord may justly be a terror to him, and he may, he ought to look upon it as that which will be the end of his course and ways. 'There is no condemnation to them that are in Christ' (Rom. 8:1).

True! But who shall have the comfort of this assertion? Who may assume it to himself? 'They that walk after the Spirit, and not after the flesh.' But you will say: Is not this to persuade men to unbelief? I answer, no: there is a twofold judgment that a man may make of himself, first, of his person, and second, of his ways: it is the judgment of his ways, not his person, that I speak of. Let a man get the best evidence for his person that he can; yet to judge that an evil way will end in destruction is his duty; not to do it, is atheism. I do not say that in such a condition a man ought to throw away the evidences of his personal interest in Christ; but I say, he cannot keep them. There is a twofold condemnation of a man's self. First, in respect of desert, when the soul concludes that it deserves to be cast out of the presence of God; and this is so far from a business of unbelief, that it is an effect of faith. Secondly, with respect to the issue and event, when the soul concludes it shall be damned. I do not say this is the duty of any one, nor do I call them to it. But this I say, that the end of an evil way wherein a man is, ought by him to be concluded to be death, that he may be provoked to fly from it. And this is another consideration that ought to dwell upon such a soul, if it desire to be freed from the entanglement of its lusts.

3. *Consider the evils of it.*

I mean its present evils: danger respects what is to come, evil what is present. Some of the many evils that attend an unmortified lust, may be mentioned.

(1) It grieves the holy and blessed Spirit, which is given
to believers to dwell in them and abide with them. So
the apostle (Eph. 4:25-29), dissuading them from many
lusts and sins, gives this as the great motive of it: 'Grieve
not the Holy Spirit, whereby you are sealed to the day
of redemption' (v. 30). Grieve not that Spirit of God,
saith he, whereby you receive so many and so great
benefits; of which he instances one signal and
comprehensive one, sealing to the day of redemption.
He is grieved by it, as a tender and loving friend is
grieved at the unkindness of his friend, of whom he
hath well deserved: so is it with this tender and loving
Spirit, who hath chosen our hearts for a habitation to
dwell in, and there to do for us all that our souls desire.
He is grieved by our harbouring in our hearts with
him, his enemies and those whom he is to destroy. He
doth not afflict willingly, nor grieve us (Lam. 3:33),
and shall we daily grieve him? Thus is he said sometimes
to be 'vexed', sometimes 'grieved at his heart', to
express the greatest sense of our provocation.

Now if there be any thing of gracious ingenuousness
left in the soul, if it be not utterly hardened by the
deceitfulness of sin, this consideration will certainly
affect it. Consider who and what thou art, who the
Spirit is that is grieved, what he hath done for thee,
what he comes to thy soul about, what he hath already
done in thee, and be ashamed. Among those who walk
with God, there is no greater motive and incentive
unto universal holiness, to the preserving of their
hearts and spirits in all purity and cleanness, than this,
that the blessed Spirit, who hath undertaken to dwell

in them as temples of God and to preserve them meet for him who so dwells in them, is continually considering what they give entertainment in their hearts unto, and rejoiceth when his temple is kept undefiled. That was a high aggravation of the sin of Zimri, that he brought his adulteress into the congregation in the sight of Moses and the rest, who were weeping for the sins of the people (Num. 25:6). And is it not a high aggravation of the countenancing a lust, or suffering it to abide in the heart when it is, as it must be if we are believers, entertained under the peculiar eye and view of the Holy Ghost, taking care to preserve his tabernacle pure and holy?

(2) The Lord Jesus is wounded afresh by it. His new creature in the heart is wounded. His love is foiled, his adversary gratified. As a total relinquishment of him by the deceitfulness of sin is the crucifying him afresh, and the putting him to open shame; so, every harbouring of sin that he came to destroy, wounds and grieves him.

(3) It will take away a man's usefulness in his generation. His works, his endeavours, his labours, seldom receive blessing from God. If he be a preacher, God commonly blows upon his ministry, so that he shall labour in the fire, and not be honoured with any success, or with doing any work for God; and the like may be spoken of other conditions. The world is at this day full of poor, withering professors: how few are there that walk in any beauty or glory! How barren,

how useless are they, for the most part! Amongst the many reasons that may be assigned of this sad estate, it may justly be feared this is none of the least effectual, that many men harbour spirit-devouring lusts in their bosoms, which lie as worms at the root of their obedience, and corrode and weaken it day by day. All graces, all the ways and means whereby any graces may be exercised and improved, are prejudiced by this means; and as to any success, God blasts such men's undertakings.

This, then, is my second direction, and it regards the opposition which is to be made to lust in respect of its habitual residence in the soul. Keep alive upon thy heart these or the like considerations of its guilt, danger and evil: be much in the meditation of these things; cause thy heart to dwell and abide upon them. Engage thy thoughts to these considerations; let them not go off, nor wander from them, until they begin to have a powerful influence upon thy soul, until they make it to tremble.

CHAPTER 11

The third direction proposed. Load the conscience with the guilt of the perplexing distemper. The ways and means whereby that may be done. The fourth direction. Vehement desire for deliverance. The fifth direction. Some distempers rooted deeply in men's natural tempers. Considerations of such distempers: ways of dealing with them. The sixth direction. Occasions and advantages of sin to be prevented. The seventh direction. The first actings of sin vigorously to be opposed.

*D*irection 3: Load thy conscience with the guilt of it. Not only consider that it hath a guilt, but load thy conscience with the guilt of its actual eruptions and disturbances.

For the right improvement of this rule, I shall give some particular directions.

(1) Take God's method in it, and begin with generals, and so descend to particulars.

[i] Charge thy conscience with that guilt which

appears in it, from the rectitude and holiness of the law. Bring the holy law of God into thy conscience; lay thy corruption to it; pray that thou mayest be affected with it. Consider the holiness, spirituality, fiery severity, inwardness, absoluteness, of the law; and see how thou canst stand before it. Be much, I say, in affecting thy conscience with the terror of the Lord in the law, and how righteous it is that every one of thy transgressions should receive a recompense of reward. Perhaps thy conscience will invent shifts and evasions to keep off the power of this consideration; as, that the condemning power of the law doth not belong to thee, that thou art set free from it and the like; and that so, though thou be not conformable to it, yet thou needest not to be so much troubled at it.

But, tell thy conscience that it cannot manage any evidence to the purpose that thou art not free from the condemning power of sin, whilst thy unmortified lust lies in thy heart; so that, perhaps, the law may make good its plea against thee for a full dominion, and then thou art a lost creature. Wherefore it is best to ponder to the utmost what it hath to say.

Assuredly, he that pleads in the most secret reserve of his heart that he is freed from the condemning power of the law, thereby secretly to countenance himself in giving the least allowance unto any sin or lust, is not able, on gospel grounds, to manage any evidence unto any tolerable, spiritual security that indeed he is, in a due manner, freed from what he so pretends himself to be delivered from.

Farther, whatever be the issue, yet the law hath commission from God to seize upon transgressors wherever it finds them, and so bring them before his throne, where they are to plead for themselves. This is thy present case; the law hath found thee out, and before God it will bring thee. If thou canst plead a pardon, well and good; if not, the law will do its work.

However, this is the proper work of the law, to discover sin in the guilt of it, to awake and humble the soul for it, to be a glass to represent sin in its colours; and if thou deniest to deal with it on this account, it is not through faith, but through the hardness of thy heart and the deceitfulness of sin.

This is a door that too many professors have gone out at, to open apostasy. Such a deliverance from the law they have pretended, as that they would consult its guidance and direction no more, they would measure their sin by it no more. By little and little this principle hath insensibly proceeded from the notion of it to influence their practical understandings; and having taken possession there, hath turned the will and affections loose to all manner of abominations.

By such ways as these, then, I say, persuade thy conscience to hearken diligently to what the law speaks in the name of the Lord unto thee, about thy lust and corruption. Oh! if thy ears be open, it will speak with a voice that shall make thee tremble, that shall cast thee to the ground, and fill thee with astonishment. If ever thou wilt mortify thy corruptions, thou must tie up thy conscience to the law, shut it from all shifts and exceptions, until it owns its guilt with a clear and thorough apprehension; so that thence, as David speaks, thy 'iniquity may be ever before thee' (Ps. 51:3).

[ii] Bring thy lust to the gospel, not for relief, but for further conviction of its guilt: look on him whom thou hast pierced, and be in bitterness. Say to thy soul, 'What have I done? What love, what mercy, what blood, what grace, have I despised and trampled on! Is this the return I make to the Father for his love, to the Son for his blood, to the Holy Ghost for his grace? Do I thus requite the Lord? Have I defiled the heart that Christ died to wash, which the blessed Spirit hath chosen to dwell in? And can I keep myself out of the dust? What can I say to the dear Lord Jesus? How shall I hold up my head with any boldness before him? Do I account communion with him of so little value, that for this vile lust's sake I have scarce left him any room in my heart? How shall I escape, if I neglect so great salvation? In the mean time, what shall I say to the Lord? Love, mercy, grace, goodness, peace, joy, consolation; I have despised them all, and esteemed them as a thing of nought, that I might harbour a lust in my heart.

'Have I obtained a view of God's fatherly countenance that I might behold his face and provoke him to his face? Was my soul washed that room might be made for new defilements? Shall I endeavour to disappoint the end of the death of Christ? Shall I daily grieve that Spirit whereby I am sealed to the day of redemption?'

Entertain thy conscience daily with this treaty. See if it can stand before this aggravation of its guilt. If this make it not sink in some measure, and melt, I fear thy case is dangerous.

(2) Descend to particulars. As, under the general head of the gospel, all the benefits of it are to be considered, such as redemption, justification and the like; so in particular, consider the management of the love that is in them toward thine own soul, for the aggravation of the guilt of thy corruption. As,

[i] Consider the infinite patience and forbearance of God towards thee in particular. Consider what advantages he might have taken against thee, to have made thee a shame and a reproach in this world, and an object of wrath for ever; how thou hast dealt treacherously and falsely with him from time to time, flattered him with thy lips, but broken all promises and engagements, and that by the means of that sin thou art now in pursuit of; and yet he hath spared thee from time to time, although thou seemest boldly to have put it to the trial how long he could hold out. And wilt thou yet sin against him? Wilt thou yet weary him, and make him to serve with thy corruptions?

Hast thou not often been ready thyself to conclude that it was utterly impossible that he should bear any longer with thee; that he would cast thee off, and be gracious no more; that all his forbearance was exhausted, and hell and wrath was even ready prepared for thee? And yet, above all thy expectation, he hath returned with visitations of love; and wilt thou yet abide in the provocation of the eyes of his glory?

[ii] How often hast thou been at the door of being hardened by the deceitfulness of sin, and by the infinite, rich grace of God hast been recovered to communion with him again!

Hast thou not found grace decaying; delight in duties, ordinances, prayer and meditation vanishing; inclinations to loose, careless walking thriving; and such as before were entangled, almost beyond recovery? Hast thou not found thyself engaged, and that with delight, in such ways, societies, companies, as God abhors? And wilt thou venture any more to the brink of hardness?

[iii] All God's gracious dealings with thee, in providential dispensations, deliverances, afflictions, mercies, enjoyments: all ought here to have a place. By these, I say, and the like means, load thy conscience, and leave it not until it be thoroughly affected with the guilt of thy indwelling corruption; until it is sensible of its wound and lie in the dust before the Lord. Unless this be done to the purpose, all other endeavours are to no purpose. Whilst the conscience hath any means to alleviate the guilt of sin, the soul will never vigorously attempt its mortification.

Direction 4

Being thus affected with thy sin, in the next place, get a constant longing and breathing after deliverance from the power of it. Suffer not thy heart one moment to be contented with thy present frame and condition. Longing desires after any thing, in things natural and civil, are of no value nor consideration any farther than as they incite and stir up the person in whom they are, to the diligent use of means for the bringing about the thing aimed at. In spiritual things it is otherwise. Longing, breathing and panting after deliverance is a grace in itself, that hath a mighty power to conform the soul into the likeness of the thing longed after. Hence the apostle, describing the repentance and godly sorrow of the Corinthians, reckons this vehement desire as one eminent grace that was then set on work (2 Cor. 7:11). And in this case of indwelling sin, and the power of it, what frame doth he express himself to be in (Rom. 7:24)? His heart breaks out with longings into a most passionate expression of desire of deliverance. Now if this be the frame of saints upon the general consideration of indwelling sin, how is it to be heightened and increased when thereunto is added the perplexing rage and power of any particular lust and corruption! Assure thyself, unless thou longest for deliverance, thou shalt not have it.

This will make the heart watchful for all opportunities of advantage against its enemy, and ready to close with any assistances that are afforded for its destruction. Strong desires are the very life of that 'praying always' which is enjoined us in all conditions, and which in none is more necessary than in this: they set faith and hope on work, and are the soul's moving after the Lord. Get thy heart into a panting and breathing frame; long, sigh, cry out. You know the example of David; I shall not need to insist on it.

Direction 5
Consider whether the distemper with which thou art perplexed, be not rooted in thy nature, and cherished, fomented and heightened from thy constitution. A

proneness to some sins may doubtless lie in the natural temper and disposition of men. In this case, consider,

(1) This is not in the least an extenuation of the guilt of thy sin. Some, with an open profaneness, will ascribe gross enormities to their temper and disposition. And whether others may not relieve themselves from the pressing guilt of their distempers by the same consideration, I know not. It is from the fall, from the original depravation of our natures, that the fuel and nourishment of any sin abides in our natural temper. David reckons his being 'shapen in iniquity and conceived in sin' (Ps. 51:5) as an aggravation of his following sin, not a lessening or extenuation of it. That thou art peculiarly inclined unto any sinful distemper, is but a peculiar breaking out of original lust in thy nature, which should peculiarly abase and humble thee.

(2) That which thou hast to fix upon on this account in reference to thy walking with God is that so great an advantage is given to sin, as also to Satan, by this thy temper and disposition that, without extraordinary watchfulness, care and diligence, they will assuredly prevail against thy soul. Thousands have been on this account hurried headlong to hell, who otherwise might at least have gone at a more gentle, less provoking, less mischievous rate.

(3) For the mortification of any distemper, so rooted in the nature of a man, in addition to all other ways and means already named or further to be insisted on, there is one expedient peculiarly suited. This is that of

the apostle, 'I keep under my body, and bring it into subjection' (1 Cor. 9:27). The bringing of the very body into subjection is an ordinance of God, tending to the mortification of sin. This gives check to the natural root of the distemper, and withers it by taking away its fatness of soil. Perhaps, because the papists (men ignorant of the righteousness of Christ, the work of his Spirit and the whole business in hand, knowing indeed the true nature neither of sin nor mortification) have laid the whole weight and stress of mortification in voluntary services and penances leading to the subjection of the body, it may, on the other side, be a temptation to some to neglect some means of humiliation which by God himself are owned and appointed. The bringing of the body into subjection in the case insisted on, by cutting short the natural appetite by means of fasting, watching and the like, is doubtless acceptable to God, if it be done with the ensuing limitations.

[i] That the outward weakening and impairing of the body be not looked upon as a thing good in itself, or that any mortification doth consist therein (which were again to bring us under carnal ordinances); but only as a means for the end proposed, the weakening of any distemper in its natural root and seat. A man may have leanness of body and soul together.

[ii] That the means whereby this is done, namely, by fasting and watching, and the like, be not looked on as things that in themselves, and by virtue of their own power, can produce true mortification of any sin; for if they would, sin might be mortified, without any

help of the Spirit, in any unregenerate person in the world. They are to be looked on only as ways whereby the Spirit may, and sometimes doth, put forth strength for the accomplishing of his own work, especially in the case mentioned. Want of a right understanding and due improvement of these and the like considerations, hath raised a mortification among the papists that may be better applied to horses and other beasts of the field than to believers.

This is the sum of what hath been spoken: when the distemper complained of seems to be rooted in natural temper and constitution, in applying our souls to a participation of the blood and Spirit of Christ, an endeavour is to be used to give check in the way of God to the natural root of that distemper.

Direction 6

Consider what occasions, what advantages, thy distemper hath taken to exert and put forth itself, and watch against them all. This is one part of that duty which our blessed Saviour recommends to his disciples under the name of watching: 'I say unto you all, watch' (Mark 13:37); which in Luke 21:34 is: 'Take heed that your hearts be not overcharged': watch against all eruptions of thy corruptions. I mean that duty which David professed himself to be exercised unto: 'I have,' saith he, 'kept myself from mine iniquity' (Ps. 18:23). He watched all the ways and workings of his iniquity in order to get before them, to rise up against them. This is that which we are called to under the name of 'considering our ways'.

Consider what ways, what companies, what opportunities, what studies, what businesses, what conditions, have at any time given, or do usually give, advantages to thy distempers; and set thyself heedfully against them all. Men will do this with respect to their bodily infirmities and distempers: the seasons, the diet, the air that have proved offensive shall be avoided. Are the things of the soul of less importance? Know that he who dares to dally with occasions of sin, will dare to sin. He that will venture upon temptations to wickedness, will venture upon wickedness. Hazael thought he should not be so wicked as the prophet told him he would be: to convince him, the prophet tells him no more but, 'Thou shalt be king of Syria' (2 Kgs. 8:13). If he will venture on temptations unto cruelty, he will be cruel. Tell a man he shall commit such and such sins, he will startle at it; if you can convince him that he will venture on such occasions and temptations to them he will have little ground left for his confidence.

Particular directions belonging to this head are many, not now to be insisted on. But because this head is of no less importance than the whole doctrine here handled, I have in another treatise about entering into temptations, treated of it at large.

Direction 7
Rise mightily against the first actings of thy distemper, its first conceptions. Suffer it not to get the least ground: do not say, 'Thus far it shall go, and no farther.' If it have allowance for one step, it will take another. It

is impossible to fix bounds to sin. It is like water in a channel; if it once break out, it will have its course. Its not acting is easier to be compassed than its bounding. Therefore doth James give that gradation and process of lust (1:14, 15), that we may stop at the entrance. Dost thou find thy corruption to begin to entangle thy thoughts? Rise up with all thy strength against it, with no less indignation than if it had fully accomplished what it aims at. Consider what an unclean thought would have; it would have thee roll thyself in folly and filth. Ask envy what it would have; murder and destruction are at the end of it. Set thyself against it with no less vigour than if it had utterly debased thee to wickedness. Without this course thou wilt not prevail. As sin gets ground in the affections to delight in it, it gets also upon the understanding to slight it.

CHAPTER 12

The eighth direction. Thoughtfulness of the excellency of the majesty of God. Our unacquaintedness with him, proposed and considered.

*D*irection 8: Use and exercise thyself to such meditations as may serve to fill thee at all times with self-abasement, and thoughts of thine own vileness. As,

(1) Be much in thoughtfulness of the excellency of the majesty of God and thine infinite, inconceivable distance from him. Many thoughts of it cannot but fill thee with a sense of thine own vileness, which strikes deep at the root of any indwelling sin. When Job comes to a clear discovery of the greatness and excellency of God, he is filled with self-abhorrency and is pressed to humiliation (Job 42:5, 6). And into what state doth the prophet Habakkuk affirm himself to be cast, upon the apprehension of the majesty of God? See chapter 3:16. 'With God,' says Job, 'is terrible majesty' (37:22).

Hence were the thoughts of them of old, that when they had seen God they should die. The Scripture abounds in this self-abasing consideration, comparing the men of the earth to 'grasshoppers', to 'vanity', to 'the dust of the balance', in respect of God (Isa. 40:13-15). Be much in thoughts of this nature, to abase the pride of thy heart, and to keep thy soul humble within thee. There is nothing will create in thee a great indisposition to be imposed on by the deceits of sin, than such a frame of heart. Think greatly of the greatness of God.

(2) Think much of thine unacquaintedness with him: though thou knowest enough to keep thee low and humble, yet how little a portion is it that thou knowest of him! The contemplation hereof cast that wise man into those apprehensions of himself which he expresses: 'Surely I am more brutish than any man, and have not the understanding of a man. I neither learned wisdom, nor have the knowledge of the holy. Who hath ascended up into heaven, or descended? Who hath gathered the wind in his fists? Who hath bound the waters in a garment? Who hath established the ends of the earth? What is his name, and what is his son's name, if thou canst tell?' (Prov. 30:2-4). Labour with this also to take down the pride of thy heart. What dost thou know of God? How little a portion is it! How immense is he in his nature! Canst thou look without terror into the abyss of eternity? Thou canst not bear the rays of his glorious being.

Because I look on this consideration as of great use in our walking with God, so far as it has (which it may have) a consistency with that filial boldness to draw nigh to the throne of grace, which is given us in Jesus Christ, I shall further insist upon it, in order to give an abiding impression of it to the souls of them who desire to walk humbly with God.

Consider then, I say, in order to keep thy heart in continual awe of the majesty of God, that persons of the most high and eminent attainments, of the nearest and most familiar communion with God, do yet in this life know but a very little of him and his glory. God reveals his name to Moses, even the most glorious attributes that he hath manifested in the covenant of grace, yet all are but the back parts of God (Exod. 34:5, 6). All that he knows by it, is but little, low, compared to the perfection of his glory.

Hence, it is with peculiar reference to Moses that it is said, 'No man hath seen God at any time' (John 1:18). Of him in comparison with Christ, doth he speak (v. 17), and of him it is here said, 'no man', no, not Moses, the most eminent among them, 'hath seen God at any time'. We speak much of God; can talk of him, his ways, his works, his counsels, all the day long: the truth is, we know very little of him; our thoughts, our meditations, our expressions of him, are low, many of them unworthy of his glory, none of them reaching his perfections.

You will say that Moses was under the law, when God wrapped up himself in darkness, and his mind in types and clouds, and dark institutions. Under the glorious shining of the gospel, which hath brought life and immortality to light, God being revealed from his own bosom, we now know him much more clearly, and as he is; we see his face now, and not his back parts only, as Moses did.

Answer 1. I acknowledge a vast and almost inconceivable difference between the acquaintance we now have with God, after his speaking to us by his own Son, and that which the generality of the saints had under the law (Heb. 1:2); for although their eyes were as good, sharp and clear as ours, their faith and spiritual understanding not behind ours, the object as glorious unto them as unto us, yet our day is more clear than theirs was; the clouds are blown away and scattered, the shadows of the night are gone and fled away, the sun is risen, and the means of sight are made more eminent and clear than formerly (Canticles 4:6).

Answer 2. Yet that peculiar sight which Moses had of God (Exod. 34) was a gospel sight, a sight of God as gracious, etc., while still it is called but his back parts, that is, but low and mean in comparison of his excellences and perfections.

Answer 3. The apostle, exalting to the utmost this glory of gospel light above that of the law, and manifesting that now the veil causing darkness is taken away, so that 'with open' or uncovered 'face we behold the glory of the Lord', tells us how we behold it, 'as in a glass' (2 Cor. 3:18). How is that? clearly, perfectly? Alas! no: he tells you how that is (1 Cor. 13:12); 'we see through a glass darkly', saith he. It is not a telescope, that helps us to see things afar off, concerning which the apostle speaks. And yet what poor helps they are! how short do we come of the truth of things, notwithstanding their assistance! It is a looking-glass whereunto he alludes, where are only obscure species and images of things, and not the things themselves; and it is a sight therein that he compares our knowledge to; he tells you also that all that we do see, by or through this glass, is 'in an enigma', in a riddle, in darkness and obscurity: and, speaking of himself, who surely was more clear-sighted than any now living, he tells us that he saw 'but in part', he saw but the back parts of heavenly things (v. 12).

And he compares all the knowledge he had attained of God to that he had of things when he was a child (v. 11); it is a part, short of that which is perfect; yea, such as shall be destroyed or done away. We know what weak, feeble, uncertain notions and apprehensions, children have of things of any abstruse consideration; how, when they grow up with any improvements of parts and abilities, those conceptions vanish, and they are ashamed of them. It is the commendation of a child to love, honour, believe and obey his father; but as for his science and notions, his father knows their childishness and folly. Notwithstanding all our confidence of high attainments, all our notions of God are but childish in respect of his infinite perfections. We, for the most part, but lisp and babble, and say we know not what, in our most accurate (as we think) conceptions and notions of God. We may love, honour, believe and obey our Father; and therewith he accepts our childish thoughts, for they are but childish. We see but his back parts; we know but little of him.

Hence is that promise, wherewith we are so often supported and comforted in our distress, 'we shall see him as he is' (1 John 3:2); we shall 'see him face to face', 'know as we are known' (1 Cor. 13:12); 'comprehend that for which we are comprehended'; that is, positively, now we see him not; all concluding that here we see but his back parts, not as he is, but in a dark, obscure representation, not in the perfection of his glory.

The Queen of Sheba had heard much of Solomon, and thereupon framed many great thoughts of his magnificence in her mind; but when she came and saw his glory, she was forced to confess that the one half of the truth had not been told her. We may suppose that we have attained here great knowledge, clear and high thoughts of God; but alas! when he shall bring us into his presence, we shall cry out, we never knew him as he is; the thousandth part of his glory, and perfection, and blessedness, never entered into our hearts.

The apostle tells us (1 John 3:2) that we know not what we ourselves shall be, what we shall find ourselves in the issue; much less will it enter into our hearts to conceive what God is, and what we shall find him to be. Consider either him who is to be known, or the way whereby we know him, and this will further appear.

(1) We know so little of God, because it is God who is thus to be known; that is, it is he who hath described himself to us very much by this, that we cannot know

him. What else doth he intend, where he calls himself invisible, incomprehensible and the like? that is, he whom we do not, cannot know as he is: and our further progress consists more in knowing what he is not, than what he is. Thus is he described to be immortal, infinite; that is, he is not as we are, mortal, finite and limited. Hence is that glorious description of him: 'Who only hath immortality, dwelling in the light which no man can approach unto, whom no man hath seen nor can see' (1 Tim. 6:16). His light is such as no creature can approach unto; he is not seen, not because he cannot be seen, but because we cannot bear the sight of him. The light of God, in whom there is no darkness, forbids all access to him by any creature whatever; we, who cannot behold the sun in its glory, are too weak to bear the beams of infinite brightness.

On this consideration, as was said, the wise man professeth himself a very beast, and not to have the understanding of a man (Prov. 30:2); that is, he knew nothing in comparison of God, so that he seemed to have lost all his understanding when once he came to the consideration of him, his work and his ways. In this consideration let our souls descend to some particulars.

As to the being of God, we are so far from a knowledge of it, so as to be able to instruct one another therein by words and expressions of it, that to frame any conceptions in our mind, with such forms and impressions of things as those whereby we receive the knowledge of all other things, is to make an idol to ourselves, and so to worship a god of our own making, and not the God that made us. We may as well, and as lawfully, hew him out of wood or stone, as form him in our minds a being suited to our apprehensions.

The utmost of the best of our thoughts of the being of God, is that we can have no thoughts of it. Our knowledge of a being is but low, when it mounts no higher than only to know that we know it not.

Again, there be some things of God which he himself hath taught us to speak of, and to regulate our expressions of them; but when we have so done, we see not the things themselves, we know them not; to believe and admire is all that we attain to. We profess, as we are taught, that God is infinite, omnipotent, eternal; and we know what disputes and notions there are about omnipresence, immensity, infiniteness and eternity. We have, I say, words and notions about these things; but as to the things themselves, what do we know, what do we comprehend of them? Can the mind of man, which is as nothing, do any more but swallow itself up in an infinite abyss? give itself up to what it cannot conceive, much less express? Is not our understanding brutish in the contemplation of such things, and as if it were not? Yea, the perfection of our understanding is not to understand, and to rest there: they are but the back parts of eternity and infiniteness that we have a glimpse of.

What shall I say of the Trinity, or the subsistence of distinct persons in the same individual essence? A mystery by many denied, because by none understood; a mystery whose every letter is mysterious. Who can declare the generation of the Son, the procession of the Spirit or the difference of the one from the other? But I shall not farther instance in particulars.

That infinite and inconceivable distance that is between him and us, keeps us in the dark as to any sight of his face, or clear apprehensions of his perfections. We know him rather by what he does, than by what he is; by his doing us good, than by his essential goodness: and how little a portion of him, as Job speaks, is hereby discovered!

(2) We know little of God, because it is faith alone whereby here we know him. I shall not now discourse about the impressions remaining on the hearts of all men by nature, that there is a God; nor what they may rationally be taught concerning that God, from the works of his creation and providence which they see and behold. It is confessedly, and that upon the woeful experience of all ages, so weak, low, dark, confused, that none ever, on that account, glorified God as they ought, but notwithstanding all their knowledge of God, were indeed without God in the world.

The chief, and (as to this matter) almost only acquaintance we have with God and his dispensations of himself, is by faith. 'He that cometh to God must believe that he is, and that he is a rewarder of them that seek him' (Heb. 11:6). Our knowledge of him and his rewarding (the foundation of our obedience or coming to him), is believing. 'We walk by faith, and not by sight' (2 Cor. 5:7); by faith, and so by faith, as not to have any express idea, image or form of that which we believe; faith is all the argument we have of things not seen (Heb. 11:1). I might here insist upon the nature of it, and manifest from all its concomitants and concernments that we know but the back parts of what we know by faith only. As to its rise, it is built purely upon the testimony of him whom we have not seen; as the apostle speaks, 'How can ye love him whom you have not seen?' that is, whom you know not but by faith that he is. Faith receives all upon his testimony, whom it receives to be, only upon his own testimony. As to its nature, it is an assent upon testimony, not an evidence upon demonstration; and, as was said before, the object of it is above us. Hence our faith, as was formerly observed, is called a seeing darkly, as in a glass; all that know this way (and all that we know of God we know this way), is but low, and dark, and obscure.

But you will say, all this is true, yet it is only so to them that, perhaps, know not God as he is revealed in Jesus Christ; with them who do so, it is otherwise. It is true, 'no man hath seen God at any time, but the only-begotten Son, he hath revealed him' (John 1:17, 18); and 'the Son of God is now come, and hath given us an understanding that we may know him that is true' (1 John 5:20). The illumination of the glorious gospel of Christ, who is the image of God, shineth upon believers (2 Cor. 4:4). Yea, and God, 'who commandeth light to shine out of darkness, shines into their hearts, to give them the knowledge of his glory in the face of his Son' (v. 6), so that 'though we were darkness, yet we are now light in the Lord' (Eph. 5:8). And the apostle says, 'we all, with open face, behold the glory of the Lord' (2 Cor. 3:18); and we are now so far from being in such darkness, or at such a distance from God, that 'our communion and fellowship is with the Father and the Son' (1 John 1:3). The light of the gospel whereby now God is revealed, is glorious; not a star, but the sun in his beauty is risen upon us, and the veil is taken from our faces; so that though unbelievers, yea, and perhaps some weak believers, may be in some darkness, yet those of any growth or considerable attainments have a clear sight and view of the face of God in Jesus Christ.

Answer 1. The truth is, we all of us know enough of him to love him more than we do, to delight in him and serve him, believe him, obey him, put our trust in him, above all that we have hitherto attained.

Our darkness and weakness are no plea for our negligence and disobedience. Who is it that hath walked up to the knowledge that he hath had of the perfections, excellences and will of God? God's end in giving us any knowledge of himself here is that we may glorify him as God; that is, love him, serve him, believe and obey him, give him all the honour and glory that is due from poor sinful creatures to a sin-pardoning God and Creator. We must all acknowledge that we were never thoroughly transformed into the image of that knowledge which we have had. And had we used our talents well, we might have been trusted with more.

Answer 2. Comparatively, that knowledge which we have of God by the revelation of Jesus Christ in the gospel is exceedingly eminent and glorious. It is so in comparison of any knowledge of God that might otherwise be attained, or was delivered under the Old Testament in the law, which had but the shadow of good things, not the express image of them. This the apostle pursues at large (2 Cor. 3). Christ hath now, in these last days, revealed the Father from his own bosom, declared his name, made known his mind, will and counsel in a far more clear, eminent, distinct manner than he did formerly whilst he kept his people under the training of the law. And this is that which, for most part, is intended in the places before mentioned; the clear, perspicuous delivery and declaration of God and his will in the gospel is expressly exalted in comparison of any other way of revelation of himself.

Answer 3. The difference between believers and unbelievers as to knowledge, is not so much in the matter of their knowledge, as in the manner of knowing. Unbelievers, some of them, may know more, and be able to say more, of God, his perfections and his will than many believers; but they know nothing as they ought, nothing in a right manner, nothing spiritually and savingly, nothing with a holy, heavenly light. The excellency of a believer is not that he hath a large apprehension of things; but that what he doth apprehend, which perhaps may be very little, he sees in the light of the Spirit of God, in a saving, soul-transforming light; and this is that which gives us communion with God, and not prying thoughts, or curious raised notions.

Answer 4. Jesus Christ, by his Word and Spirit, reveals to the hearts of all his, God as a Father, as a

God in covenant, as a rewarder, and that in a manner every way sufficient to teach us to obey him here, and to lead us to his bosom, to lie down there in the fruition of him to eternity. But yet, now,

Answer 5. Notwithstanding all this, it is but a little portion we know of him; we see only his back parts. For,

[i] The intention of all gospel revelation is not to unveil God's essential glory, so that we should see him as he is, but merely to declare so much of him as he knows to be a sufficient foundation of our faith, love, obedience and coming to him; that is, of the faith which here he expects from us, of such services as become poor creatures in the midst of temptations. But when he calls us to eternal admiration and contemplation without interruption, he will make a new manner of discovery of himself; and the whole shape of things, as it now lies before us, will depart as a shadow.

[ii] We are dull and slow of heart to receive the things that are in the Word revealed; God, by our infirmity and weakness, keeping us in continual dependence on him for teachings and revelations of himself out of his Word, and never in this world bringing any soul to the utmost of what is from the Word to be made out and discovered; so that, although the way of revelation in the gospel be clear and evident, yet we know little of the things themselves that are revealed.

Let us then revive the use and intention of this consideration. Will not a due apprehension of this inconceivable greatness of God, and that infinite distance wherein we stand from him, fill the soul with a holy and awful fear of him, so as to keep it in a frame unsuited to the thriving or flourishing of any lust whatever? Let the soul be continually used to reverential thoughts of God's greatness and omnipresence, and it will be much upon its watch as to any undue deportments. Consider him with whom you have to do; even 'our God is a consuming fire'; and in your greatest abashments at his presence and eye, know that your very nature is too narrow to bear apprehensions suitable to his essential glory.

CHAPTER 13

*The ninth direction. When the heart is disquieted by
sin, speak no peace to it, until God speak it. Peace without
detestation of sin, unsound; so is peace, measured and
unto ourselves. How we may know when we measure our
peace unto ourselves. Directions as to that inquiry. The
vanity of speaking peace slightly. Also of doing it on
one singular account, not universally.*

*D*irection 9. In case God disquiet the heart about
the guilt of its distempers, either in respect of
its root and indwelling, or in respect of any
eruptions of it, take heed that thou speakest not peace
to thyself before God speaks it; but hearken what he
says to thy soul. This is our next direction, without the
observation whereof the heart will be exceedingly
exposed to the deceitfulness of sin.

This is a business of great importance. It is a sad
thing for a man to deceive his own soul herein. All the
warnings God gives us, in tenderness to our souls, to
try and examine ourselves, do tend to the preventing

of this great evil of speaking peace groundlessly to ourselves; which is, as to the issue, to bless ourselves in an opposition to God. It is not my business to insist upon the danger of it, but to help believers to prevent it, and to let them know when they do so.

To manage this direction aright, observe:

(1) That, as it is the great prerogative and sovereignty of God to give grace to whom he pleases (he hath mercy 'on whom he will' [Rom. 9:16], and among all the sons of men, he calls whom he will, and sanctifies whom he will); so, among those so called and justified, and whom he will save, he yet reserves this privilege to himself, to speak peace to whom he pleaseth, and in what degree he pleaseth, even amongst them on whom he hath bestowed grace. He is 'the God of all consolation' in an especial manner in his dealings with believers. That is one of the good things that he keeps locked up in his family, and of it gives out to all his children at his pleasure. This the Lord insists on (Isa. 57:16-18); it is the case under consideration that is there insisted on. When God says, he will heal their breaches and disconsolations, he assumes this privilege to himself in an especial manner. 'I create it' (v. 19): even in respect of these poor wounded creatures, I create it, and, according to my sovereignty, make it out as I please.

Hence, as it is with the conferring of grace in reference to them who are in the state of nature, that God doth it in great peculiarity, and his proceedings therein, in taking and leaving, are as to outward appearances quite beside, and oftentimes contrary to, all probable expectations; so is it in his communication of peace and joy in reference to them that are in the state of grace; he gives them out oftentimes quite beside our expectation, as to any appearing grounds of his dispensations.

(2) As God creates it for whom he pleases, so it is the prerogative of Christ to speak it home to the conscience. Speaking to the church of Laodicea, who had healed her wounds falsely, and who spoke peace to herself when she ought not, he takes to himself that title, 'I am the Amen, the faithful witness' (Rev. 3:14). He bears testimony concerning our condition, as it is indeed. We may possibly mistake, and trouble ourselves in vain, or flatter ourselves upon false grounds; but he is the Amen, the faithful witness; and what he speaks of our state and condition, that it is indeed. He is said not to judge according to the sight of the eye; not according to any outward appearance, or any thing that may be subject to a mistake, as we are apt to do; but he shall judge and determine every cause as it is indeed (Isa. 11:3).

Take these two previous observations, and I shall give some rules whereby men may know whether God speaks peace to them, or whether they speak peace to themselves only.

(1) Men certainly speak peace to themselves, when their so doing is not attended with the greatest detestation imaginable of that sin, in reference

whereunto they do speak peace to themselves, and with abhorrency of themselves for it. When men are wounded by sin, disquieted and perplexed, and, knowing that there is no remedy for them but only in the mercies of God through the blood of Christ, do therefore look to him and to the promises of the covenant in him; and thereupon quiet their hearts that it shall be well with them, and that God will be exalted that he may be gracious to them; while yet their souls are not wrought to the greatest detestation of the sin or sins on account whereof they are disquieted; this is to heal themselves, and not to be healed of God. This is but 'a great and strong wind' that the Lord is nigh unto, but the Lord is not in the wind. When men do truly look upon Christ whom they have pierced, without which there is no healing or peace, they will mourn (Zech. 12:10); they will mourn for him even upon this account, and detest the sin that pierced him. When we go to Christ for healing, faith eyes him peculiarly as one pierced.

Faith takes several views of Christ, according to the occasions it hath of address to him and communion with him. Sometimes it views his holiness, sometimes his power, sometimes his love, his favour with his Father. And when it goes for healing and peace, it looks especially on the blood of the covenant, on his sufferings; for by his stripes we are healed, and 'the chastisement of our peace was upon him' (Isa. 53:5). When we look for healing, his stripes are to be eyed; not in the outward story of them, which is the course of popish devotionists, but in the love, kindness, mystery and design of the cross. And when we look for peace, his chastisement must be in our eye.

Now I say that this, if it be done according to the mind of God, and in the strength of that Spirit which is poured out on believers, will beget a detestation of that sin or sins for which healing and peace are sought. So Ezekiel 16:60, 61: 'Nevertheless I will remember my covenant with thee in the days of thy youth, and I will establish unto thee an everlasting covenant.' And what then? 'Then thou shalt remember thy ways and be ashamed.' When God comes home to speak peace in a sure covenant of it, it fills the soul with shame for all the ways whereby it hath been alienated from him.

And one of the things that the apostle mentions, as attending that godly sorrow which is accompanied with repentance unto salvation never to be repented of, is revenge; 'Yea, what revenge!' (2 Cor. 7:11). They reflected on their miscarriages, with indignation and revenge for their folly in them. When Job comes up to a thorough healing, he cries, 'Now I abhor myself' (Job 42:6); and until he did so, he had no abiding peace. He might, perhaps, have made up himself with that doctrine of free grace which was so excellently preached by Elihu (33:14-30); but he would then have but skinned his wounds: he must come to self-abhorrency if he would come to healing. So was it with those in Psalm 78:33, 35, in their great trouble and perplexity for and upon account of sin. I doubt not, but, upon the address they made to God in Christ (for that so they did is evident from the titles they gave him, they call him their Rock and their Redeemer,

two words everywhere pointing out the Lord Christ),
they spake peace to themselves. But was it sound and
abiding? No, it passed away as the early dew: God
speaks not one word of peace to their souls. But why
had they not peace? Why, because in their address to
God they flattered him. But how doth that appear?
'Their heart was not right with him, neither were they
stedfast' (v. 37). They had not a detestation nor
relinquishment of that sin, in reference whereunto they
spake peace to themselves.

Let a man make what application he will for healing
and peace; let him do it to the true Physician, let him
do it the right way, let him quiet his heart in the
promises of the covenant; yet when peace is spoken, if
it be not attended with the detestation and abhorrency
of that sin which was the wound, and caused the
disquietment, this is no peace of God's creating, but
of our own purchasing. It is but a skinning over the
wound, whilst the matter of it lies at the bottom, which
will putrefy, and corrupt, and corrode, until it break
out again with noisomeness, vexation and danger.

Let not poor souls that walk in such a path as this;
that are more sensible of the trouble of sin than of the
pollution or uncleanness that attends it; that address
themselves for mercy, yea, to the Lord in Christ address
themselves for mercy, but yet will keep the sweet
morsel of their sin under their tongue; let them not, I
say, ever think to have true and solid peace.

For instance, thou findest thy heart running out
after the world, and it disturbs thee in thy communion
with God. The Spirit speaks expressly to thee, 'He that

loveth the world, the love of the Father is not in him' (1 John 2:15). This puts thee on dealing with God in Christ for the healing of thy soul, the quieting of thy conscience; but yet withal a thorough detestation of the evil itself abides not upon thee; yea, perhaps, that is liked well enough, except only in respect of the consequences of it. Perhaps thou mayest be saved, yet, as through fire, and God will have some work with thee before he hath done: but thou wilt have little peace in this life; thou wilt be sick and fainting all thy days (Isa. 57:17).

This is a deceit that lies at the root of the peace of many professors, and wastes it. They deal with all their strength about mercy and pardon, and seem to have great communion with God in their so doing; they lie before him, so bewail their sins and follies that any one would think, yea, they think themselves that surely they and their sins are now parted; and so they receive in mercy that satisfies their hearts for a little season. But when a thorough search comes to be made, there hath been some secret reserve for the folly or follies treated about; at least, there hath not been that thorough abhorrency of it which is necessary; and their whole peace is quickly discovered to be weak and rotten, scarce abiding any longer than the words of begging it are in their mouths.

(2) When men measure out peace to themselves upon the conclusions to which their convictions and rational principles will carry them, this is a false peace, and will not abide. I shall a little explain what I mean hereby.

A man hath got a wound by sin, he hath a conviction of some sin upon his conscience; he hath not walked uprightly as becometh the gospel; all is not well and right between God and his soul. He considers now what is to be done. Light he hath, and knows what path he must take, and how his soul hath been formerly healed. Considering that the promises of God are the outward means of application for the healing of his sores and quieting of his heart, he goes to them, searches them out, finds out some one or more of them whose literal expressions are directly suited to his condition. Says he to himself, 'God speaks in this promise; here I will take myself a plaster as long and broad as my wound'; and so he brings the word of the promise to his condition, and sets him down in peace. This is another appearance upon the mount; the Lord is near, but the Lord is not in it. It hath not been the work of the Spirit, who alone can convince us of sin and righteousness and judgment (John 16:8), but the mere actings of the intelligent, rational soul.

There are, we say, three sorts of lives, the vegetative, the sensitive, and the rational or intelligent; some things have only the vegetative; some the sensitive also, and that includes the former; some have the rational, which takes in and supposes both the others. Now he that hath the rational doth not only act suitably to that principle, but also to both the others; he grows and is sensible. It is so with men in the things of God: some are mere natural and rational men; some have a superadded conviction with illumination; and some are truly regenerate. Now he that hath the latter, hath also the former; and therefore he acts sometimes upon the principles of the rational, sometimes upon the principles of the enlightened man. His true, spiritual life is not the principle of all his motions; he acts not always in the strength thereof, neither are all his fruits from that root.

In this case that I speak of, he acts merely upon the principle of conviction and illumination, whereby his first natural powers are heightened; but the Spirit breathes not at all upon all these waters.

Take an instance: suppose the wound and disquiet of the soul to be upon account of relapses, than which there is nothing whereby deeper wounds are given to the soul, nor greater disquietments, whatever the evil or folly be, though never so small as to the matter of it. In the perturbation of his mind, he finds out that promise: 'The LORD will have mercy, and our God will abundantly pardon' (Isa. 55:7), that is, he will multiply or add to pardon, he will do it again and again; or that in Hosea 14:4: 'I will heal their backsliding, I will love them freely'. This the man considers, and thereupon concludes peace to himself, whether the Spirit of God make the application or no, whether that give life and power to the letter or no: that he regards not. He doth not hearken whether God the Lord speak peace. He doth not wait upon God, who perhaps yet hides his face, and sees the poor creature stealing peace and running away with it; knowing that the time will come when he will deal with him again, and call him to a new reckoning (Hos. 11:3); when he shall see that it is in vain to go one step where God doth not take him by the hand.

I see here, indeed, sundry other questions upon this arising and interposing themselves: I cannot apply myself to them all; one I shall a little speak to.

Question. It may be said, then: Seeing that this seems to be the path that the Holy Spirit leads us in, for the healing of our wounds and quieting of our hearts, how shall we know when we go alone ourselves, and when the Spirit also doth accompany us?

Answer 1. If any of you are out of the way upon this account, God will speedily let you know it; for, besides that you have his promise, that 'the meek he will guide in judgment, and teach them his way' (Ps. 25:9), he will not let you always err. He will, I say, not suffer your nakedness to be covered with fig-leaves, but take them away, and all the peace you have in them, and will not suffer you to settle on such lees; you shall quickly know your wound is not healed. That is, you shall speedily know by the event whether or no it be thus with you; the peace you thus get and obtain will not abide. Whilst the mind is overpowered by its own convictions, there is no hold for disquietments to fix upon; stay a little, and all these reasonings will grow cold, and vanish before the face of the first temptation that arises. But,

Answer 2. This course of speaking peace is commonly taken without waiting, which is the grace, and that peculiar acting of faith, which God calls for to be exercised in such a condition. I know God doth sometimes come in upon the soul instantly, in a moment as it were, wounding and healing it; as I am persuaded it was in the case of David when he cut off the lap of Saul's garment; but ordinarily, in such a case, God calls for waiting and labouring, attending as the eye of a servant upon his master (Ps. 123:2; 130:6). Says the prophet Isaiah (8:17), 'I will wait upon the LORD, who hideth his face from Jacob.' God will have his children lie a while at his door when they have run from his house, and not instantly rush in upon him; unless he take them by the hand and pluck them in, when they are so ashamed that they dare not come to him. Now self-healers, or men that speak peace to themselves, do commonly make haste; they will not tarry; they do not hearken to what God speaks (Isa. 28:16), but on they will go to be healed.

Answer 3. Such a course, though it may quiet the conscience and the mind, the rational, concluding part of the soul, yet doth not sweeten the heart with rest and gracious contentment. The answer it receives is much like that Elisha gave Naaman, 'Go in peace' (2 Kgs. 5:19); it quieted his mind, but I much question whether it sweetened his heart, or gave him any joy in believing other than the natural joy that was then stirred in him upon his healing. 'Do not my words do good? saith the Lord' (Mic. 2:7). When God speaks, not only is there truth in his words that may answer the conviction of our understanding, but also they do good, they bring that which is sweet and good and desirable to the will and affections; by them the soul returns unto its rest (Ps. 116:7).

Answer 4. Which is worst of all, such a course amends not the life, it heals not the evil, it cures not the distemper. When God speaks peace, it guides and keeps the soul that it turn not again to folly (Ps. 85:8). When we speak it ourselves, the heart is not taken off the evil. Nay, it is the readiest course in the world to bring a soul into a trade of backsliding. If upon thy plastering thyself, thou findest thyself rather animated to the battle again than utterly weaned from it, it is too palpable that thou hast been at work with thy own soul, but Jesus Christ and his Spirit were not there. Yea, and oftentimes, nature having done its work, will, ere a few days are over, come for its reward; and having been active in the work of healing, will be ready to reason for the new wounding. In God's speaking peace, there comes along so much sweetness, and such a discovery of his love, as is a strong obligation on the soul no more to deal perversely.

(3) We speak peace to ourselves when we do it slightly. This the prophet complains of in some teachers: 'They have healed the wound of the daughter of my people slightly' (Jer. 6:14). And it is so with some persons; they make the healing of their wounds a slight work; a look, a glance of faith to the promises does it, and so the matter is ended. The apostle tells us, that the word did not profit some, because it was not 'mixed with faith' (Heb. 4:2); that is, it was not well tempered and mingled with faith. It is not a mere look to the word of mercy in the promise; but it must be mingled with faith until that be incorporated into the very nature of it; and then indeed it doth good unto the soul. If thou hast a wound upon thy conscience, which was attended with weakness and disquietness, which now thou art

freed of, how camest thou so? 'I looked to the promises of pardon and healing, and so found peace.' Yea, but perhaps thou hast made too much haste; thou hast done it superficially; thou hast not fed upon the promise, so as to mix it with faith, to have got all the virtue of it diffused into thy soul. Thou hast only done it slightly; thou wilt find thy wound, ere it be long, breaking out again; and thou shalt know that thou art not cured.

(4) Whoever speaks peace to himself upon any one account, and at the same time hath another evil of no less importance lying upon his spirit, about which he hath had no dealing with God: that man cries peace when there is none. A little to explain my meaning: a man hath neglected a duty again and again, perhaps when in all righteousness it was due from him; his conscience is perplexed, his soul wounded; he hath no quiet in his bones by reason of his sin; he applies himself for healing, and finds peace. Yet in the mean time, perhaps, worldliness, or pride, or some other folly wherewith the Spirit of God is exceedingly grieved, may lie in the bosom of that man, and they neither disturb him, nor he them. Let not that man think that any of his peace is from God.

Then shall it be well with men when they have an equal respect to all God's commandments. God will justify us from our sins, but he will not justify the least sin in us; he is a God of purer eyes than to behold iniquity.

(5) When men of themselves speak peace to their consciences, it is seldom that God speaks humiliation

to their souls: God's peace is humbling peace, melting peace, as it was in the case of David (Ps. 51:1). Never such deep humiliation, as when Nathan brought him the tidings of his pardon.

Question. But you will say: When may we take the comfort of a promise as our own in relation to some peculiar wound, for the quieting of the heart?

Answer. In general, when God speaks it; be it when it will, sooner or later. I told you before, he may do it in the very instant of the sin itself, and that with such irresistible power, that the soul must needs receive his mind in it. Sometimes he will make us wait longer; but when he speaks, be it sooner or later, be it when we are sinning or repenting, be the condition of our souls what they please, if God speak he must be received. There is not any thing in our communion with him, for which the Lord is more troubled with us, if I may so say, than our unbelieving fears that keep us off from receiving that strong consolation which he is so willing to give to us.

Question. But you will say: We are where we were; when God speaks it, we must receive it; that is true, but how shall we know when he speaks?

Answer 1. I would we could all practically come up to this, to receive peace when we are convinced that God speaks it, and that it is our duty to receive it: but,

Answer 2. There is, if I may so say, a secret instinct in faith, whereby it knows the voice of Christ when he speaks indeed; as the babe leaped in the womb when the blessed virgin came to Elisabeth, faith leaps in the heart when Christ indeed draws nigh to it. 'My sheep,' says Christ, 'know my voice' (John 10:14); they know my voice, that is, they are used to the sound of it; and they know when his lips are opened to them, and are full of grace. The spouse was in a sad condition, asleep in security (Canticles 5:2); but yet as soon as Christ speaks, she cries, 'It is the voice of my Beloved that speaks.' She knew his voice, and was so acquainted with communion with him that instantly she discovers him. And so will you also: if you exercise yourselves to acquaintance and communion with him, you will easily discern between his voice and the voice of a stranger. And take this criterion with you: when he doth speak, he speaks as never man spake; he speaks with power; and, one way or other, will make your hearts burn within you, as he did to the disciples (Luke 24:32). He doth it by putting in his hand at the hole of the door (Canticles 5:4): that is, his Spirit into your hearts, to seize on you.

He that hath his senses exercised to discern good and evil, being increased in judgment and experience by a constant observation of the ways of Christ's intercourse, the manner of the operations of the Spirit, and the effects it usually produces, is the best judge for him in this case.

Answer 3. If the word of the Lord doth good to your souls, he speaks it. If it humble, if it cleanse, and be useful for those ends for which promises are given, such as to endear, to cleanse, to melt and bind to obedience, to cause self-emptiness, etc. But this is not my business; nor shall I further divert in the pursuit of this direction, without the observation of which, sin will have great advantages towards the hardening of the heart.

CHAPTER 14

The general use of the foregoing directions. The great direction for the accomplishment of the work aimed at. Act faith on Christ: the several ways whereby this may be done. Consideration of the fulness in Christ for relief, proposed. Great expectations from Christ: grounds of these expectations; his mercifulness, his faithfulness. Event of such expectations; on the part of Christ; on the part of believers. Faith peculiarly to be acted on the death of Christ (Rom. 6:3-6). The work of the Spirit in this whole business.

Now, the considerations which I have hitherto insisted on are rather of things preparatory to the work aimed at, than such as will affect it. That which hitherto I have aimed at is the heart's due preparation for the work itself, without which it will not be accomplished.

Directions for the work itself
These are very few; I mean such as are peculiar to it. And they are those that follow.

Direction 1. Set faith at work on Christ for the killing of thy sin. His blood is the great sovereign remedy for sin-sick souls. Live in this, and thou wilt die a conqueror. Yea, thou wilt, through the good providence of God, live to see thy lust dead at thy feet. But thou wilt say: How shall faith act itself on Christ for this end and purpose? I say, sundry ways.

(1) By faith fill thy soul with a due consideration of that provision which is laid up in Jesus Christ; for this end and purpose that all thy lusts, this very lust wherewith thou art entangled, may be mortified by faith. Ponder on this, that though thou art no way able, in or by thyself, to get the conquest over thy distemper; though thou art even weary of contending, and art utterly ready to faint (Luke 18:1, 7); yet that there is enough in Jesus Christ to yield thee relief (Phil. 4:13). It stayed the prodigal when he was ready to faint, that yet there was bread enough in his father's house; though he was at a distance from it, yet it relieved him, and stayed him, that there it was. In thy greatest distress and anguish, consider that fulness of grace, those riches, those treasures of strength, might and help, that are laid up in him for our support (John 1:16; Col. 1:19; Isa. 40:28-31). Let them come into and abide in thy mind.

Consider that he is exalted, and made a Prince and a Saviour, to give repentance unto Israel (Acts 5:31). And if to give repentance, to give mortification, without which the other is not, nor can be. Christ tells us that we obtain purging grace by abiding in him (John

15:3). To act faith upon the fulness that is in Christ for our supply, is an eminent way of abiding in Christ, for both our ingrafting and abode is by faith (Rom. 11:19, 20).

Let, then, thy soul be exercised by faith with such thoughts and apprehensions as the following. I am a poor, weak creature; unstable as water, I cannot excel. This corruption is too hard for me, and is at the very door of ruining my soul; and what to do I know not. My soul is become as parched ground, and a habitation of dragons. I have made promises and broken them; vows and engagements have been as a thing of nought. Many persuasions have I had that I had got the victory and should be delivered; but I am deceived; so that I plainly see, that without some eminent succour and assistance, I am lost, and shall be prevailed on to an utter relinquishment of God. But yet, though this be my state and condition, let the hands that hang down be lifted up, and the feeble knees be strengthened. Behold the Lord Christ, who hath all fulness of grace in his heart, all fulness of power in his hand (John 1:16; Matt. 28:18): he is able to slay all these his enemies. There is a sufficient provision in him for my relief and assistance: he can take my drooping, dying soul, and make me more than a conqueror (Rom. 8:38).

Why sayest thou, O my soul, 'My way is hid from the LORD, and my judgment is passed over from my God? Hast thou not known, hast thou not heard, that the everlasting God, the LORD, the Creator of the ends of the earth, fainteth not, neither is weary; there is no searching of his understanding; he giveth power to the faint, and to them that have no might he increaseth strength. Even the youths shall faint and be weary, and the young men shall utterly fall; but they that wait upon the LORD shall renew their strength; they shall mount up with wings as eagles, they shall run, and not be weary, they shall walk, and not faint' (Isa. 40:27-31).

He can make the dry, parched ground of my soul to become a pool, and my thirsty, barren heart as springs of water; yea, he can make this habitation of dragons, this heart so full of abominable lusts and fiery temptations, to be a place for grass and fruit for himself (Isa. 35:7).

So God stayed Paul under his temptation, with the consideration of the sufficiency of his grace: 'My grace is sufficient for thee' (2 Cor. 12:9). Though he were not immediately made partaker of it so far as to be freed from his temptation, yet the sufficiency of it in God for that end and purpose, was enough to stay his spirit. I say then, by faith be much in the consideration of that supply, and the fulness of it that is in Jesus Christ; and how he can at any time give thee strength and deliverance. Now, if hereby thou dost not find success to a conquest, yet thou wilt be stayed in the chariot that thou shalt not fly out of the field until the battle be ended; thou wilt be kept from any utter despondency and a lying down under thy unbelief, or a turning aside to false means and remedies that in the issue will not relieve thee. The efficacy of this consideration will be found only in the practice.

(2) Raise up thy heart by faith to an expectation of relief from Christ. Relief in this case from Christ is like the prophet's vision (Hab. 2:3): it is 'for an appointed time, but at the end it shall speak, and not lie; though it tarry, yet wait for it, because it will surely come, it will not tarry.' Though it may seem somewhat long to thee whilst thou art under thy trouble and perplexity, yet it shall surely come in the appointed time of the Lord Jesus, which is the best season. If, then, thou canst raise up thy heart to a settled expectation of relief from Jesus Christ; if thine eyes are towards him as 'the eyes of a servant to the hand of his master' (Ps. 123:2), when he expects to receive somewhat from him; thy soul shall be satisfied (Isa. 7:4, 7-9). He will assuredly deliver thee; he will slay the lust, and thy latter end shall be peace: only look for it; at his hand expect when and how he will do it. 'If you will not believe, surely ye shall not be established.'

Question. But thou wilt say: What ground have I to build such an expectation upon, so that I may expect not to be deceived?

Answer. As thou hast necessity to put thee on this course, and must be relieved and saved this way or none (To whom wilt thou go? John 6:68); so there are in the Lord Jesus innumerable things to encourage and engage thee to this expectation.

As for the necessity of it, I have in part discovered it before, when I manifested that this is the work of faith, and of believers only. 'Without me,' says Christ, 'you can do nothing', speaking with especial relation to the purging of the heart from sin (John 15:2, 5). Mortification of any sin must be by a supply of grace. Of ourselves we cannot do it. Now it hath pleased the Father 'that in Christ all fulness should dwell' (Col. 1:19); that 'of his fulness we might receive grace for grace' (John 1:16). He is the Head, from whence the new man must have influences of life and strength, or it will decay every day. If we are 'strengthened with might' in the inner man (Col. 1:11), it is by Christ's 'dwelling in our hearts by faith' (Eph. 3:16, 17). That this work is not to be done without the Spirit, I have also showed before. Whence do we expect the Spirit? From whom do we look for him? Who hath promised him to us, having procured him for us? Ought not all our expectations to this purpose to be on Christ alone? Let this then be fixed upon thy heart, that if thou hast not relief from him, thou shalt never have any; all ways, endeavours, contendings that are not animated by this expectation of relief from Christ and him only are to no purpose, will do thee no good; yea, if they are any thing else than supportments of thy heart in this expectation, or means appointed by himself for the receiving help from him, they are in vain.

Now, further to engage thee to this expectation,

[i] Consider his mercifulness, tenderness and kindness as he is our great High Priest at the right hand of God. Assuredly he pities thee in thy distress: saith he, 'As one whom his mother comforteth, so will

I comfort you' (Isa. 66:13): he hath the tenderness of a mother to a sucking child.

> Wherefore in all things it behoved him to be made like unto his brethren, that he might be a merciful High Priest in things pertaining to God, to make reconciliation for the sins of the people; for in that he himself hath suffered, being tempted, he is able to succour them that are tempted (Heb. 2:17, 18).

How is the ability of Christ upon the account of his suffering here proposed to us? 'In that he himself hath suffered, being tempted, he is able.'

Did the sufferings and temptations of Christ add to his ability and power? Not, doubtless, considered absolutely and in itself; but the ability here mentioned is such as hath readiness, proneness, willingness to put itself forth, accompanying it. It is an ability of will against all dissuasions; he is able, having suffered and being tempted, to break through all dissuasions to the contrary, to relieve poor, tempted souls. He is 'able' to help; it is a word taken from the effect; for he can now be moved to help, having been so tempted. So chapter 4:15, 16:

> For we have not an High Priest which cannot be touched with the feeling of our infirmities, but was in all points tempted like as we are, yet without sin: let us therefore come boldly to the throne of grace, that we may obtain mercy, and find grace to help in time of need.

The exhortation of verse 16, is the same that I am upon, namely, that we would entertain expectations of relief from Christ, which the apostle there calls 'grace for seasonable help'. If ever, says the soul, help were seasonable, it would be so to me in my present condition: this is that which I long for, grace for seasonable help; I am ready to die, to perish, to be lost for ever; iniquity will prevail against me if help come not in. Says the apostle, 'Expect this help, this relief, this grace from Christ.' Yea, but on what account? That he lays down (v. 15): and we may observe, that the word (v. 16), which we have translated 'to obtain' means 'that we may receive it'; suitable and seasonable help will come in. I shall freely say this one thing, that establishing the soul by faith in expectation of relief from Jesus Christ (Matt. 11:28), on account of his mercifulness as our High Priest, will be more available to the ruin of thy lust and distemper, and have a better and speedier issue than all the rigidest means of self-maceration that ever any of the sons of men engaged themselves in. Yea, let me add, that never any man did or shall perish by the power of any lust, sin or corruption, who could raise his soul by faith to an expectation of relief from Jesus Christ (Isa. 55:1-3; Rev. 3:18).

[ii] Consider his faithfulness who hath promised; which may raise thee up and confirm thee in this waiting in an expectation of relief. He hath promised to relieve in such cases, and he will fulfil his Word to the utmost. God tells us that his covenant with us is like the ordinances of heaven, the sun, moon and stars,

which have their certain courses (Jer. 31:36). Thence
David said, that he watched for relief from God, as
one watcheth for the morning, a thing that will
certainly come in its appointed season; so will be thy
relief from Christ. It will come in its season, as the
dew and rain upon the parched ground; for faithful is
he who hath promised. Particular promises to this
purpose are innumerable; with some of them, that
seem peculiarly to suit his condition, let the soul be
always furnished.

Now, there are two eminent advantages which
always attend this expectation of succour from Jesus
Christ.

(i) It engages him to a full and speedy assistance.
Nothing doth more engage the heart of a man to be
useful and helpful to another, than his expectation of
help from him, if justly raised, and countenanced by
him who is to give the relief. Our Lord Jesus Christ
hath, by his kindness, care and promises, raised our
hearts to this expectation; certainly our rising up to it
must needs be a great engagement upon him to assist
us accordingly. This the psalmist gives us as an approved
maxim: 'Thou, Lord, never forsakest them that put
their trust in thee'. When the heart is once won to
rest in God, to repose itself on him, he will assuredly
satisfy it. He will never be as water that fails, nor hath
he 'said at any time to the seed of Jacob, Seek ye my
face in vain' (Isa. 45:19). If Christ be chosen for the
foundation of our supply, he will not fail us.

(ii) It engages the heart to attend diligently to all
ways and means whereby Christ is wont to comm-

unicate himself to the soul, and so takes in the real assistance of all graces and ordinances whatever. He that expects any thing from a man, applies himself to the ways and means whereby it may be obtained. The beggar that expects an alms, lies at his door or in his way from whom he doth expect it. The way whereby, and the means wherein, Christ communicates himself is and are, ordinarily, his ordinances. He that expects any thing from him must attend upon him therein. It is the expectation of faith that sets the heart to work. It is not an idle, groundless hope that I speak of. If, now, there be any vigour, efficacy and power in prayer or sacraments to this end of mortifying sin, a man will assuredly be interested in it all by this expectation of relief from Christ. On this account I reduce all particular actings, by prayer, meditation and the like, to this head; and so shall not further insist on them. When they are grounded on this bottom, and spring from this root, they are of singular use to this purpose: and not else.

Now on this direction for the mortification of a prevailing distemper you may have a thousand proofs from experience. Who hath walked with God under this temptation, and hath not found the use and success of it? I dare leave the soul under it, without adding any more. Only some particulars relating thereunto may be mentioned.

(1) Act faith peculiarly upon the death, blood and cross of Christ: that is, on Christ as crucified and slain. Mortification of sin is peculiarly from the death of Christ. It is one peculiar, yea, eminent end of the death

of Christ, which shall assuredly be accomplished by it. He died to destroy the works of the devil; whatever came upon our natures by his first temptation, whatever receives strength in our persons by his daily suggestions, Christ died to destroy it all. 'He gave himself for us, that he might redeem us from all iniquity, and purify unto himself a peculiar people, zealous of good works' (Titus 2:14). This was his aim and intention, wherein he will not fail, in his giving himself for us. That we might be freed from the power of our sins, and purified from all our defiling lusts, was his design. 'He gave himself for the church, that he might sanctify and cleanse it, that he might present it to himself a glorious church, not having spot or wrinkle, or any such thing, but that it should be holy and without blemish' (Eph. 5:25-27).

And this, by virtue of his death, in various and several degrees, shall be accomplished. Hence, our washing, purging and cleansing, is every where ascribed to his blood (1 John 1:7; Heb. 1:3; Rev. 1:5). That being sprinkled on us, 'purges our consciences from dead works, to serve the living God' (Heb. 9:14). This is that we aim at, this we are in pursuit of, that our consciences may be purged from dead works; that these may be rooted out, destroyed and have place in us no more. This shall certainly be brought about by the death of Christ; there will virtue go out from thence to this purpose. Indeed, all supplies of the Spirit, all communications of grace and power, are from hence, as I have elsewhere showed (*Treatise on Communion with God*, chs 7, 8).

Thus the apostle states it (Rom. 6). In verse 2, is the case proposed that we have in hand; 'How shall we that are dead unto sin, live any longer therein?' Dead to sin by profession; dead to sin by obligation to be so; dead to sin by a participation of virtue and power for the killing of it; dead to sin by union and interest in Christ, in and by whom it is killed; how shall we live therein? This he presses in the ensuing verses by sundry considerations, all taken from the death of Christ. This must not be: 'Know you not, that so many of us as were baptised into Jesus Christ were baptised into his death?' (v. 3). We have in baptism an evidence of our implantation into Christ; we are baptised into him; but into what of him are we baptised in order to an interest therein? His death, saith he: if indeed, and beyond outward profession, we are baptised into Christ, we are baptised into his death. The explication of this, of our being baptised into the death of Christ, the apostle gives us:

> Therefore we are buried with him by baptism into death, that like as Christ was raised up from the dead by the glory of the Father, even so we also should walk in newness of life: knowing this, that our old man is crucified with him, that the body of sin might be destroyed, that henceforth we should not serve sin (vv. 4, 5).

This is, saith he, our being 'baptised into the death of Christ', namely, our conformity thereunto; to be dead unto sin, to have our corruptions mortified, as he was put to death for sin; so that as he was raised up to glory, we may be raised up to grace and newness of life.

He tells us whence it is that we have this baptism into the death of Christ, and this is from the death of Christ itself: 'Our old man is crucified with him, that the body of sin might be destroyed' (v. 6). 'Is crucified with him', not in respect of time, but of causality: we are crucified with him, meritoriously, in that he procured the Spirit for us to mortify sin; efficiently, in that from his death virtue comes forth for our crucifying; in the way of a representation and exemplar; we shall assuredly be crucified unto sin, as he was for our sin. This is that the apostle intends. Christ, by his death, destroying the works of the devil, procuring the Spirit for us, hath so killed sin as to its reign in believers, that it shall not obtain its end and dominion.

(2) Then, act faith on the death of Christ, and that under these two notions: [i] In expectation of power; [ii] In endeavours for conformity (Phil. 3:10; Col. 3:3; 1 Pet. 1:15-19).

For the first, the direction given in general may suffice.

As to the latter, the words of the apostle (Gal. 3:1) may give us some light unto our direction. Let faith look on Christ in the gospel as he is set forth dying and crucified for us; look on him under the weight of our sins, praying, bleeding, dying; bring him in that condition into thy heart by faith; apply his blood, so shed, to thy corruptions; do this daily (1 Cor. 15:31; 1 Pet. 1:16; 5:1, 2; Col. 1:3). I might draw out this consideration to a great length, in sundry particulars, but I must come to a close.

I have only, then, to add the heads of the work of the Spirit in this business of mortification, which is so peculiarly ascribed to him. In one word, this whole work which I have described as our duty, is affected, carried on and accomplished by the power of the Spirit, in all the parts and degrees of it. As,

(1) He alone clearly and fully convinces the heart of the evil, and guilt, and danger of the corruption, lust or sin to be mortified. Without this conviction, or whilst it is so faint that the heart can wrestle with it or digest it, there will be no thorough work made. An unbelieving heart (as, in part, we all have such) will shift with any consideration, until it be overpowered by clear and evident convictions: now this is the proper work of the Spirit; he convinces of sin (John 16:8). He alone can do it. If men's rational considerations, with the preaching of the letter, were able to convince them of sin, we should, it may be, see more convictions than we do. There comes, by the preaching of the Word, an apprehension upon the understandings of men that they are sinners, that such and such things are sins, that themselves are guilty of them; but this light is not powerful, nor doth it lay hold on the practical principles of the soul, so as to conform the mind and will unto them, and to produce effects suitable to such an apprehension. And therefore it is, that wise and

knowing men, destitute of the Spirit, do not think those things to be sins at all wherein the chief movings and actings of lust do consist. It is the Spirit alone that can do, that doth, this work to the purpose. And this is the first thing that the Spirit doth in order to the mortification of any lust whatever; he convinces the soul of all the evil of it, cuts off all its pleas, discovers all its deceits, stops all its evasions, answers its pretences, makes the soul own its abomination and lie down under the sense of it. Unless this be done, all that follows is in vain.

(2) The Spirit alone reveals unto us the fulness of Christ for our relief: which is the consideration that stays the heart from false ways, and from despairing despondency (2 Cor. 12:8, 9).

(3) The Spirit alone establishes the heart in expectation of relief from Christ: which is the great sovereign means of mortification, as hath been discovered (2 Cor. 1:21, 22).

(4) The Spirit alone brings the cross of Christ into our hearts, with its sin-killing power; for by the Spirit are we baptised into the death of Christ.

(5) The Spirit is the Author and Finisher of our sanctification: gives new supplies and influences of grace for holiness and sanctification, when the contrary principle is weakened and abated (Eph. 3:16-18).

(6) In all the soul's addresses to God in this condition, it hath supportment from the Spirit. Whence is the power, life and vigour of prayer? Whence its efficacy to prevail with God? Is it not from the Spirit? He is the 'Spirit of supplication' promised to them who look on him whom they have pierced (Zech. 12:10): enabling them to pray with sighs and groans that cannot be uttered (Rom. 8:16). This is confessed to be the great medium, or way, of faith's prevailing with God. Thus Paul dealt with his temptation, whatever it were: 'I besought God that it might depart from me' (2 Cor. 12:8). What is the work of the Spirit in prayer; whence and how it gives us its assistance, and makes us to prevail; what we are to do that we may enjoy his help for that purpose; it is not my present intention to demonstrate.